TARGET
Comprehension

5

© **B. Jain Publishers (P) Ltd.** All rights reserved. No part of this book may be reproduced, stored in a retrieval system or transmitted, in any form or by any means, mechanical, photocopying, recording or otherwise, without any prior written permission of the publisher.

Published by Kuldeep Jain for B. Jain Publishers (P) Ltd., D-157, Sector 63, Noida - 201307, U.P
Registered office: 1921/10, Chuna Mandi, Paharganj, New Delhi-110055

Printed in India

Objectives of Comprehension

It is a fact that when students attempt a comprehension exercise, they are seldom aware of the purpose of the whole exercise. Many a time, even the guardians and teachers are not clear about the purpose. Of course, we are all well informed about the common purposes like comprehension teaches students to maintain their concentration level and to use strategies to enhance understanding of the reading material. Given below are some of the common objectives of comprehension:

- *Getting to understand the main idea of the text*
- *Noting the correct sequence of the happenings*
- *Recognizing the key words*
- *Making reasonable and logical conclusion*
- *Recognizing the genre of the text*
- *Distinguishing fiction from non-fiction*
- *Distinguishing fantasy from realism*
- *Recognizing the theme, plot and characters of the given passage*

What is it to monitor one's own comprehension?

Children should be trained to monitor their own comprehension from a very early age. While attempting a passage, they should read it again and again till its meaning is clear to them. They should note down the text which is not clear to them and try out to understand its meaning. They should stop regularly while reading and make sure that they fully understand what they are reading. They should reread and think again and again. They should read to the end of the passage, think sincerely and see if they are still confused. If yes, they should again read the passage and keep on reading till there confusion is vanished. They should learn the strategy of decoding multi-syllabic words and be able to summarize a variety of texts.

The series **Target Comprehension** is an excellently planned and graded series which brings together a diverse range of passages for the children to read. All the reading material that occurs in this series is judged on the basis of theme, language and the overall readability of the passages. The activities are graded and fit in justly with the passages.

Contents

1. The Adventures of Pinocchio 6
2. The King and the Squirrel 12
3. A Bicycle Built for Two 17
4. Joan of Arc 22
5. The Salt Seller and the Fox 27
6. Postage Stamp 34
7. Amazon River 39
8. Treasure Island 46
9. Alice in Wonderland 52
10. The Owl and the Pussy-Cat 58
11. Stone Flower 64
12. Birds of Paradise 69
13. The Sword in the Stone 74
14. The Four Dragons 80
15. Neil Armstrong 86
16. The Honest Merchant 91
17. The Bermuda Triangle 95
18. Camera 101
19. At the Zoo 106
20. The Pied Piper of Hamelin 111
21. Octopus 118
22. Tom Sawyer 122
23. Stopping by Woods on a Snowy Evening 129
24. Yellowstone National Park 133
25. The Four Puppets 138
26. Africa 144

Fun to Know

A warming up discussion
- What is a puppet?
- Do you help your parents in their work? How?

The Adventures of Pinocchio

Geppetto, a toy maker, once thought of making a puppet. With that idea, he went to his friend Antonio, a carpenter.

'Friend, I need a log of wood to carve a puppet,' Geppetto said.

'I have a log of magic wood,' said Antonio. Thinking that his friend must be joking, Geppetto laughed and said, 'I will take it anyway.'

When Geppetto returned home, he took his tools and started carving a puppet from the wood. First, he carved the puppet's head, then added a pair of eyes. When Geppetto looked at it, the eyes blinked! 'I must have imagined that,' Geppetto said. Then he carved the puppet's nose, which grew longer and longer! 'What's happening? This log of wood is indeed magical,' Geppetto cried in wonder.

Finally, Geppetto completed the puppet and named him Pinocchio. Geppetto loved him like his own son but Pinocchio was very naughty. Once, when Geppetto scolded Pinocchio, he ran out of the house. Pinocchio created so much mischief in the town that poor Geppetto

was jailed as he ran after him, causing more disturbance than the puppet. But soon Pinocchio was ashamed of his actions.

Next day, when Geppetto was released from prison, Pinocchio apologized to him for his mistakes. He promised that he would become a good boy and would start going to school. One day on his way to school, Pinocchio saw a puppet show. He was so impressed that he joined the puppets and entertained the crowd. The puppet master was very happy with Pinocchio's performance and rewarded him five gold coins.

On the way, Pinocchio met two crooks—a cat and a fox. They took the money that Pinocchio had earned forcefully and left him hanging from a tree branch. Pinocchio was helpless. Luckily, a fairy came to his rescue.

The fairy took Pinocchio to her castle. She gave a medicine to Pinocchio to drink to help him feel better. But Pinocchio hated medicines. So he lied, 'I have had it already.'

The next moment, Pinocchio's nose grew out like a long wooden peg. The fairy laughed and said, 'Pinocchio, whenever you lie your nose will grow.'

Soon, Pinocchio's nose was all well and he felt better. He thanked the fairy for her kindness and returned to Geppetto and told him all that had happened. He rejoined his school and made many friends. One day, one of his friends named Lampwick told him about a place called Toyland.

'It's a land of toys, Pinocchio. Will you accompany me to Toyland tonight?' asked Lampwick. Pinocchio willingly agreed.

At midnight, a coach pulled by six donkeys arrived. The coach was filled with many children and Lampwick and Pinocchio joined them.

Pinocchio had a great time in Toyland. Time passed. One morning, when Pinocchio woke up, he saw to his horror that he had become a donkey. He was taken to a circus and forced to perform tricks. 'I have been so foolish,' he lamented. When, Pinocchio failed to amuse the audience, he was thrown into the sea. Surprisingly, the moment Pinocchio fell into the sea, he once again turned into a puppet. He was happy. Suddenly a huge whale came towards him and swallowed him up!

After recovering from the shock, Pinocchio noticed that there was some sort of light inside the whale. He walked towards it and saw Geppetto sitting at a table. Geppetto was thrilled to see Pinocchio. 'I have been searching you everywhere ever since you left. Where have you been?' he asked Pinocchio. 'I was looking for you in the sea when this whale swallowed me.'

Soon, Geppetto and Pinocchio began thinking of a way to escape from the whale's stomach. They walked towards the whale's mouth, and were pleased to find that the whale had fallen asleep with its mouth wide open. Just then, a huge wave came and swept them out. Miraculously, they found an empty boat in the sea and returned home.

This time, Pinocchio actually kept his promise and became an obedient boy. He helped Geppetto in his work. One morning, when Pinocchio looked into the mirror, he was surprised to see a boy looking back at him. 'I'm a real boy now,' he cried as he rushed into Geppetto's room. When Geppetto saw Pinocchio, he cried with joy, 'It's all because of your goodness Pinocchio.'

 **Let's remember the story**

Answer the following questions.

1. What was special about the wood that Geppetto had brought?
2. Why did Geppetto land up in prison?

3. How did the fox and the cat trick Pinocchio?
4. What happened when Pinocchio started living in Toyland?
5. Why did Pinocchio become a real boy?

Practise writing sentences

Use the following words in your own sentences.

1. Puppet
   ....
2. Mistake
   ....
3. Trouble
   ....
4. Light
   ....
5. Escape
   ....
6. Empty
   ....

Pick the correct answer

Choose the correct answers from the multiple choices given.

1. Who asked Pinocchio to change his wicked ways?
   a. Geppetto

b. A talking cricket

c. A fairy

2. Why did Pinocchio's nose become long?

    a. He had told a lie

    b. He had stolen

    c. He had escaped school

3. What did Pinocchio become in Toyland?

    a. A monkey

    b. A donkey

    c. A boy

4. Whom did Pinocchio find inside the whale?

    a. The fairy

    b. The fox

    c. Geppetto

Design your own puppet

Make your own puppet using fresh materials or waste materials. Give it a name. Then write down the steps how you made it.

....

....

....

....

....

....

....

....

Let's hear your thoughts

Why do you think Pinocchio turned into a real boy at the end of the story?

....

....

....

....

....

....

....

....

....

Fun to Know

A warming up discussion
- Did you ever boast?
- What did you boast about?

The King and the Squirrel

Once upon a time, there was a proud king. He was young, well-educated, intelligent and matchless in strength and valour. He was also the richest king in the land. One day, he was taking a walk in the garden with a wise, old minister.

Suddenly, the king said, 'I am sure no one would ever dare to boast before me. I am glad to be superior to everybody in every respect.'

The old minister, who generally agreed with the young king, did not reply. Surprised, the king asked, 'Why, my good minister, do you keep quiet?'

The minister smiled and replied, 'My noble Lord, pardon me but you can never be sure that no one will ever boast before you. Often, it is seen that a weakling considers himself the boldest of knights. Similarly, one day, someone ignorant of your superiority may boast before you. It would be wise to ignore him. To take notice of others' vanity is to lose one's own peace of mind.'

Just as the minister was talking, a tiny squirrel hurried past them and climbed a marble column that stood before them. In its front paws, it held a gold coin. The king was amused. Seeing the king's smile, the squirrel chanted, 'I have got so much wealth. How much has the King? Pity how he eyes me with jealousy and suffering!'

Hearing this, the king was furious. He rushed towards the squirrel but it slipped away. In its hurry, the squirrel dropped her coin. The king pocketed that coin and was satisfied.

Later, the king was discussing important matters with the ambassadors of

the neighbouring kingdoms when suddenly, the king heard a chant. It was the squirrel sitting near the window.

'If the king is so rich and so proud, it is with my wealth; I disclose this aloud!' chanted the squirrel. The king was enraged but in front of his distinguished guests, he controlled his anger. The others heard the squirrel too but they all kept quiet. When alone, the king kept thinking about the squirrel's chanting.

Now, the king always began his day by giving alms to the poor. He likewise, was distributing alms the next morning, when again the squirrel appeared near the palace door and chanted,

'How proudly he distributes alms! But is it not my wealth that adorns his palms?'

The king commanded his attendants to capture the squirrel. But the squirrel managed to slip away. The poor king had to conceal his anger once again. In this manner, the squirrel continued to annoy the king for days, sometimes when he sat dining, sometimes when he was in meeting and sometimes when he was discussing his finances. One day, the king had had enough. When the squirrel came to chant, in his anger, the king threw a gold coin towards the squirrel. In no time, the squirrel collected the gold coin.

Then, the squirrel quickly climbed the window sill, paused and chanted, 'Victory to myself, the mighty squirrel! To all the people I can tell, the king did return all my wealth, out of fear of my strength!'

Hearing this, like a mad man the king sprang at the squirrel on the windowsill. But the swift squirrel once again left the king disappointed. At night, the hurt king was unable to sleep as the taunts of the squirrel haunted him.

In the morning, he told the minister, 'I have decided to summon all my soldiers and order them to kill all the squirrels in my kingdom.'

Hearing this, the minister said, 'My Lord, I understand your anger. But I don't think that the soldiers will manage to kill the squirrels. There may be millions of them in our kingdom. Our brave soldiers may feel insulted if they have to fight against squirrels. Then, if by chance, the naughty squirrel, which is teasing you, escapes, all our efforts will be wasted. And think of what the historians will write about you? That once upon a time, there was a king who led his army against squirrels!'

'What should I do then?' asked the dejected king.

'My Lord, simply ignore the squirrel. If you had paid no attention to the idle boasts of the squirrel in the beginning, then you wouldn't have been upset.'

The king followed the minister's advice. So when next time the squirrel came to taunt him, he did not react. In the end, the squirrel gave up troubling the king. He was happy for his minister had taught him a valuable lesson.

Let's remember the story

Answer the following questions.
1. Name a few qualities of the king.
2. Why did the king think that no one would boast before him?
3. What did his minister say regarding boasting?
4. What song did the squirrel sang when the king sat eating with his guests?
5. Why did the king want to get rid of all the squirrels in his kingdom?
6. What lesson did the king learn at the end of the story?

Can you match the words and their antonyms given in the following table?

Words	Antonyms
Quiet	Release
Succeed	Reveal
Idle	Loud
Conceal	Timid
Bold	Busy
Capture	Fail

 **Prepositions**

Fill in the blanks using the prepositions given below.

| beyond | by | over | during | down | against |

15

1. The flock of sparrows flew .... the trees.
2. He came .... the office in a great hurry.
3. The Robinsons live .... that street.
4. The boat is sailing .... the wind.
5. The cat sitting on the branch was .... his reach.
6. It rained heavily .... the night.

✓ Complete the sentences

Read the sentences given below and complete them with the help of the chapter.

1. The king thought that no one would................. before him.
2. The king picked up the.............. when the squirrel had dropped it.
3. The squirrel chanted .... when she lost her wealth.
4. The king was........................ by the squirrel's behaviour.
5. The minister asked the king to................... the chants of the squirrel.
6. The king had learnt a............................. lesson.

Let's hear your thoughts

Why do you think the king reacted the way he did when the squirrel boasted before him?

....

....

....

....

Fun to Know

A warming up discussion
- Do you know how to ride a bicycle?
- Share your experiences while learning to ride a bicycle.

A Bicycle Built for Two

There was an ambitious young eel

Who determined to ride on a wheel;

But try as he might,

He couldn't ride right,

In spite of his ardour and zeal.

If he sat on the saddle to ride

17

His tail only pedalled one side;
And I'm sure you'll admit
That an eel couldn't sit
On a bicycle saddle astride.
Or if he hung over the top,
He could go, but he never could stop;
For of course it is clear
He had no way to steer,
And under the wheel he would flop.
His neighbour, observing the fun,
Said, 'I think that the thing can be done,
If you'll listen to me,
You'll quickly agree
That two heads are better than one.
'And this is my project, old chap,
Around our two waists I will wrap
This beautiful belt
Of bottle-green felt
And fasten it firm with a strap.'
This done, with a dignified mien
The two squirmed up on the machine,
And rode gayly away,
Or at least, so they say,
Who witnessed the wonderful scene.

(Carolyn Wells)

 **Complete the sentences**

Read the sentences given below and complete them with the help of the poem.

1. The determined eel wanted ....
   ....

2. When the eel sat on the saddle ....
   ....

3. The neighbour of the eel said ....
   ....

4. The eel wrapped their waists ....
   ....

 **Words and their meanings**

Read the words given below. With the help of a dictionary find out their meanings and write in the table.

Words	Meanings
Ardour	
Zeal	
Astride	
Dignified	
Squirm	
Witness	

✓ Pick the correct answer

Choose the correct answers from the multiple choices given.

1. What was the eel trying to do?
    a. Trying to cook
    b. Trying to ride a bicycle
    c. Trying to climb

2. What could it not reach?
    a. The road
    b. Both the saddle
    c. The paddle

3. Who wanted to ride with the eel?
    a. His neighbour
    b. His aunt
    c. His cousin

4. What was the colour of the belt?
    a. Red
    b. Bottle green
    c. Black

🔍 Find friends

Match the words in Column A with their rhyming words in Column B.

20

Column A	Column B
Wheel	Peer
Flop	Glee
Firm	Keen
Scene	Term
Agree	Slop
Steer	Steel

Fun to Know

A warming up discussion
- Who is a hero?
- Can you name a national hero?

Joan of Arc

Joan of Arc is a folk heroine of France. She lived a very short life but it was full of events that changed the times that she lived in. Joan of Arc was born in Domrémy, France. She was a peasant girl. As a young girl, she used to go to the farm with his father where he worked. Her father also worked as a village official and he collected taxes. She also learnt from her mother to sew and spin. She never went to a school. Joan was very religious. Interestingly, Joan of Arc is also known as the 'Maid of Orleans'.

Joan was 12 years old, when she had a vision. In her vision, she saw St. Michael, St. Catherine and St. Margaret. The saints instructed her to drive out the English and to bring the Dauphin Charles to Reims to be crowned as the king. Dauphin was a title used by the eldest son of the king of France, who was heir to the throne of France. After this first vision, Joan continued to have many more visions. When she was 16 years old, she decided that it was now time for her to fulfil the mission that the saints had asked her.

Deciding that it was time to take action, Joan went to meet Robert de Baudricourt, who was commander of the garrison of Charles Dauphin. But he did not take her seriously and asked her to return home. But Joan had not given up. She went again to Baudricourt. This time she predicted the defeat of the French in a battle near Orleans. And it happened likewise. It was only then that Baudricourt took her seriously.

Joan went to meet Dauphin Charles at Chinon disguised as a man through the hostile territory of the Burgindians. When she met Dauphin Charles, she impressed him and asked his permission to travel with the army dressed as a knight. The Dauphin was reluctant at first but hoped that she was a messenger from God that could give them hope and perhaps a victory and he agreed. Interestingly, Dauphin dressed himself as a courtier when Joan came to meet him to fool her but she recognized him.

Her brothers Jean and Pierre too joined the army. Her standard was painted with an image of Christ, and the banner had the name of Jesus. She was then sent to the city of Orleans which was under attack from the English. By this time, it became known that she had visions and people too hoped that she was sent to save them from the English. She led the French valiantly against the English and fought bravely. She was even wounded in her neck by an arrow during this battle but she continued to fight. The French were inspired by her and they won the Battle of Orleans. Joan cut her hair short and wore armour to look like a man!

After they had had this victory, she convinced the French that they need to win the city of Reims where the French kings were crowned. The French won Reims under her leadership. Then, Joan fulfilled the second part of her vision and Dauphin Charles was crowned the king of France. During the coronation, Joan was given the place of honour next to the king.

After a French king was sitting on the throne, Joan tried to take Paris under the French control. During this battle, a crossbow severely wounded her leg but she continued to fight. Later, during the Battle of Compiègne, Joan was captured by the Burgundians. She was put in a prison and she tried to escape a number of times but remained unsuccessful. Joan was then sold to the English. Did you know that while she was in prison and her trial had started, King Charles did not try to save her?

It was then that the English tried to prove in a trial against her that she was a witch and had used witchcraft to defeat them. Representatives of the Church repeatedly interrogated her but they were unable to find anything wrong with her except that she wore a man's clothes. Later she was sentenced to die and she was burned at stake on May 30, 1431 in Rouen. She was only nineteen years old.

Later in 1456, Pope Calixtus III declared that Joan of Arc was not guilty. He also condemned the verdict that was given against her. Joan was declared a saint by the Catholic Church in 1920. She is now the patron saint of France and is considered a national heroine.

 **Let's remember the story**

Answer the following questions.

1. As a young girl what had Joan learnt?
2. What was the vision of Joan at 12 years of age?
3. How did the Dauphin tried to fool Joan?
4. What was the importance of the city of Reims?
5. What were the charges against Joan?
6. In what year and by whom was Joan of Arc declared a saint?

 **Circling the words**

Read the passage given below carefully and put a circle around the verbs.

24

In 1274, Italian explorers Marco and Niccolo Polo set out on a 24 year journey. During this time, they travelled the famous Silk Road from Italy. They crossed brutal deserts and towering mountains to reach eastern China, 4,000 miles away from Italy. Marco and Niccolo were among the very first Europeans to explore the fabled empire of China. There, Marco Polo even worked for Kublai Khan. Polo wrote in detail about his experiences and findings in China in a book.

In his writings, he described the materials and inventions that were never seen before in Europe. Paper money, a printing press, porcelain, gunpowder and coal were among the products that he wrote about. He also described the vast wealth of Kublai Khan as well as the geography of northern and southern China. When European rulers read about these inventions, they were very interested in them. They wanted these products for themselves. But, trading along the Silk Road was dangerous, expensive and impractical. And then in their craving for these things, the European rulers started to wonder if there was a sea route that led to the east.

Synonyms

Match the words with their synonyms given in the following table.

Words	Synonyms
Collect	Overcome
Instruct	At fault
Defeat	Pick up
Victory	Teach
Guilty	Conquer

 **Word grid**

Find the given words in the grid below.

| Joan | Dauphin | France | Reims |

A	E	T	P	A	T	H	F	M
U	I	F	P	I	P	S	R	F
I	S	A	S	D	J	O	A	N
D	A	U	P	H	I	N	N	D
Q	I	I	H	A	A	K	C	S
A	N	T	Y	B	B	U	E	D
R	T	H	E	E	O	I	N	A
S	S	H	R	E	I	M	S	U

 **Let's hear your thoughts**

Write a few lines about another international female leader or patriot. Tell us about her achievements.

....

....

....

....

....

....

....

Fun to Know

A warming up discussion
- Do you believe in witches?
- Have you ever seen something strange?

The Salt Seller and the Fox

One evening, a salt seller was returning home, after a long day. Suddenly, the weather became bad. In no time, dark clouds engulfed the sky and thunder and lighting flashed and soon it began to rain in torrents. The salt seller, in time, saw a giant boulder beneath which he saw a small cave. He hurried towards the cave, hoping no animal lived there. Soon, he was fast asleep.

Suddenly, an eerie sound was heard over the pouring rain. Startled, the salt seller woke up. Again, he heard the sound. Trembling with fear, he looked out of the cave for the source of the sound but saw nothing. When he heard the sound yet again, he realised that it was a woman's soft voice.

The fact that it was a human voice comforted him but he felt that something was not right. He crept out of the cave and the sound seemed to come from some place. He looked up, to the top of the giant boulder, to find the source of the voice, and what he saw filled him with great fear.

The rain had stopped by now and the clouds too had dispersed a little.

By the dim moonlight, he saw a white fox on the boulder with something white between her paws. The fox ground the object on the boulder while it mumbled to itself in a woman's voice. Looking closely, he realized that it was a human skull. The salt seller was terrified. But he quietly crawled behind a tree from where he could watch the fox without being seen. The white fox ground the skull for some time and then put it on her skull. It fitted her perfectly.

What he saw next was horrific. The fox flipped itself backwards, head-over-tail, once, twice, and then suddenly there was no fox. An old woman with a bent back stood there. She said, 'I'm late. I must hurry.' The next moment, she leaped down from the boulder and walked on the path towards the neighbouring village.

Despite his fear, the salt seller followed the old woman keeping his distance. When she had reached the village, she went directly to the house of Old Kim, the richest man in the valley. 'I'm here!' the old woman called from the gate, and the house was suddenly abuzz. Servants ran out to open the gate. They seemed to be expecting her because they led her to the wife's guest room.

Minutes later, the salt seller went to the gate and asked if he could stay the night. The servants took him in as he was a familiar face. Later, as he lay on the mat all he heard were low sounds coming from the women's room across the courtyard. Suddenly there came the loud sound of a gong, and then a voice — unmistakably that of the old woman — chanting strange incantations. The voice would die down, stop, and then the gong would strike again to begin another round of chanting. The salt seller was unable to make out the words but he was certain that the words were evil.

Just then, a servant came in to sleep. From him, the salt seller learnt that Old Kim had fallen mysteriously ill. No medicine has been able to cure him. At last, they had called on the old grandmother, a local shamaness who was known to be a good healer. But the salt seller knew that this was no shamaness. He realised that the white fox had killed the shamaness.

Thinking thus, the salt seller mustered his will and crept across the courtyard to the women's room, where the old crone's chanting had died down to a low murmur. Quietly, he sat against the sliding door and he could hear her clearly now. Though the rhythm seemed to be a traditional invocation, the words were evil and twisted.

Gently, he poked a hole in the paper panel of the door, being careful not to make a sound. He put his eye against the hole and peeked inside. He saw Old Kim asleep along with his family before the shamaness, who chanted and rhythmically tapped the brass gong by the light of an oil lamp. Suddenly, she licked her thin lips with her red tongue. Then, the salt seller saw her unusually sharp teeth and the fox's tongue.

The salt seller now knew that he must save Old Kim. Yet he knew that if he told the household that the old woman was a fox, no one would believe him. Fox demons were wily, cunning and clever, and he was a simple man of few words.

Suddenly, without thinking, he barged inside the room, crying, 'Awake! Awake!' At once, the people of the household woke up startled. Then, he ran outside to the courtyard and returned with a heavy two-headed pestle. And before anybody could stop him, he smashed the old crone's head with the pestle. The people in the room rushed forward now, too late, to restrain him, but they drew back when they heard the strange barking sounds that issued from the old woman's throat.

In a moment, what lay on the floor was no longer an old woman but a white fox wearing a cracked human skull. Old Kim's family looked on dumbfounded as the salt seller bent down and removed the grisly mask from the fox's crushed head. And now he told them what he had seen that night on the mountain.

The next morning, Old Kim had recovered as mysteriously as he had fallen ill. Out of his gratitude, he rewarded the salt seller with a portion of his wealth. After that day, the salt seller no longer had to sell salt in the mountains.

 **Let's remember the story**

Answer the following questions.

1. Where did the salt seller take shelter from the storm?

2. What did he see when he woke up?

3. What happened when the fox put the skull on its head?

4. Who was the fox pretending to be?

5. What was the plan of the fox?

6. How did the salt seller get rid of the fox?

Phrases, here we come!

Read the sentences below carefully and complete them with help of the phrases given in the box.

bury the hatchet	crocodile tears	four corners of the earth
tall story	against the grain	a feather in one's cap

1. Tim went .... and won scholarship.
2. The boy cried .... when he was caught stealing.
3. In the camp, children told each other a .... about their adventures in the forest.
4. The brothers .... and lived together again.
5. My father has travelled ....
6. Winning the race was another .... Ted's ....

Think and fill

Read the following sentences. Fill in the blanks using the correct articles, *a*, *an*, and *the*.

1. Someone call .... policeman!
2. Sarah wants .... dog for her birthday.
3. At the zoo, I saw .... elephant and ....orangutan.
4. I would like to sail over .... Mediterranean Sea.

5. Gary is .... Irishman.

6. .... Andes Mountains are in South America.

7 .... spacecraft was sent into .... space.

8. Mrs Button bought .... dozen apples.

Practise writing sentences

Use the following words in your own sentences.

1. Cave

   ....

2. Fear

   ....

3. Dim

   ....

4. Strange

   ....

5. Hole

   ....

6. White

   ....

Synonyms

Match the words with their synonyms given in the following table.

Words	Synonyms
Fearful	Rich
Night	Appreciation
Wealthy	The time after sunset and before sunrise
Gratitude	Afraid

Fun to Know

6 A warming up discussion
- Have you ever pasted a postage stamp on a letter?
- What did the postage stamp you used look like?

Postage Stamp

Each time we write a letter, we make sure that we have placed the right stamps on it. Have you ever asked your parents why they place different stamps on an envelope? Did you ever try to find out why and when the postage stamp was invented? Do you know what did the first stamp look like? Well, Rowland Hill had invented the postage stamp and it was first used on May 6, 1840.

A postage stamp is a small rectangular piece of paper that is placed on an envelope cover to show that the payment for the postage has been made. Interestingly, postage stamps are sometimes in rectangular and circular shapes as well. Usually, stamps are made from a special paper, with a national designation and its price on the face, and a gum adhesive on the reverse side. When the envelope with the stamp on it is processed at the post office, a postmark is placed on it which prevents from the stamp being reused. The postmark indicates the date and point of origin of the mail or letter. The mailed item is then delivered to the address that the customer has written on the envelope or cover.

Rowland Hill was a teacher and an administrator at schools operated by his father, in Birmingham, England. One day, he overheard a conversation where a young woman in tears was begging the postman to give her the letter from her fiancé. But the postman refused to do so because she was unable to pay the postage due. It was so because before the stamps were invented, the cost of mail was generally paid by the recipient. Also, the rates of the postage were so high that only a few people could use the service. Further, the rates of the postage were calculated according to the distance, the number of pages involved and the weight of the postage, making the rates complicated. Envelopes were rarely used in postage as the envelope was also counted as a page and it further increased the cost of the postage.

This incident made Rowland think about postage reforms. In 1837, he at last published Post Office Reform — Its Importance and Practicability. Through his reforms, he proposed the sale of postage stamps. He described the postage stamp as 'a small stamped detached label — say about an inch square — which, if prepared with a glutinous wash on the back, may be affixed.' Hill also proposed to keep the rates of stamps low, suggesting 'penny cost'. He also suggested that the postal rates should be decreased and that the frequency of postal delivery should be increased. He even said that the charge of a postal stamp should remain the same all over England and that the deliveries should be charged according to their weight only.

In his reforms, he suggested that the sender should pay the price of the letter. He pointed out that by doing thus would improve efficiency as the postal carriers would not have to wait, as they did then, for the recipients to receive the letters.

It took a long time for the proposal of Rowland Hill to be approved by the Postmaster General. But in the end the hard work and efforts of Hill were rewarded and Hill's proposals were passed into a law on 5 December 1839. These laws took effect from 6 May 1840. Did you know that the world's first stamp featured the portrait of Queen Victoria!

The first stamp was sold for one penny and now even poor people could write letters. The first stamp, One Penny Black, had no perforations to it and people had to cut each stamp using scissors from a sheet of stamps. Almost at once the volume of England's mail had doubled and it doubled again within a few years. The postal service was booming! Did you know that when the postage stamps had started, it had no glue at its back and so it was sewed or pinned to the postage! By the 1860s, about 70 countries had launched their stamps. Interestingly, Great Britain is the only country in the world that does not have its name printed on the stamp!

Collecting stamps was popular from the start but during the 1920s it actually became a craze. Stamp collection is still a popular hobby today. The variety of stamps and the history, culture, and story they tell still draws people from all walks of life to take up their tongs, get a stamp album, and start collecting stamps. Did you know that in 1973, Bhutan had issued a group of postage stamps that had folksongs recorded on one side which could be played on a record player! Fascinating, isn't it?

 **Let's remember the story**

Answer the following questions.

1. Who had invented the postage stamp and when was it first used?
2. What incident led Hill to invent stamps?
3. Write any two postage reforms.
4. Which was the first stamp?
5. What was the advantage of placing stamps on letters for the postman?
6. What were the immediate benefits of placing stamps on letters?

Prepositions

Fill in the blanks using the preposition given below.

| on | under | inside | among | at | with | until | across |

1. Mother kept all the clothes........................... the cupboard.
2. The cat is hiding.................. the table.
3. Fiona went................ her friends to the mall.
4. I will not go out.................... it stops raining.
5. His house is.............. the street.
6. The bird was sitting................ the pile of boxes.
7. The camp instructor said that there was a thief..................... us.
8. We stopped....... the pet shop on our way to the skiing ring.

Synonyms

Match the words with their synonyms given in the following table.

Words	Synonyms
Adhesive	Rebuilt
Affix	Painting
Cost	Sticky
Portrait	Mixture
Variety	Fasten
Reform	Price

37

 **Paste stamps!**

Search and collect the stamps that are available in your home and paste them in your notebook. Divide the stamps according to different sections, e.g., birds, animals, flowers, people etc.

 **The world of stamps**

After you have collected stamps, tell us how many different kinds of stamps have you found. Were there a few stamps that caught your eye? What was special about these stamps?

....
....
....
....
....
....
....
....
....
....

Fun to Know

7

A warming up discussion
- Have you seen a river? What was it like?
- Did you try fishing or boating in the river?

Amazon River

The Amazon River is the second longest river in the world. You would ask what is so special about this particular river. Well, the Amazon River is among the most important rivers in the world. Think of how much water you use in one day or even one year! Consider how much water a swimming pool contains and how long you will take to fill it! Do you know that the amount of water that Amazon River pours into the Atlantic Ocean in one second is enough to fill 2000 swimming pools with a capacity of 30,000 gallons each!

Amazingly, the Amazon River contains water equivalent to the combined waters of the Mississippi, the Nile and the Yangtze. This mighty river is 4,080 miles long and it flows in South America. The Amazon is the biggest river in the world in terms of the water it contains. The Amazon pours about 60 million gallons or 620,000 cubic yards of water i.e. freshwater into the Atlantic Ocean per second! As this massive amount of water falls into the Atlantic Ocean, it minimizes the saltiness of the sea water for up to 100 miles!

This is not all. The enormous amount of freshwater that flows out of the Amazon each day is equivalent to 12 years worth of water used by the city of New York that is every faucet, every shower, every toilet and all other combined sources of freshwater consumed by millions of people living in the city! Do you know that the Amazon contains 1/5 of the freshwater that is available on Planet Earth!

The Amazon is also the widest river in the world. It can be 6.8 miles wide at some points during the dry season but during the rainy season, this giant river can be 24.8 miles wide! It is because of the enormous amounts of water in it that the delta region through which the Amazon River empties into the Atlantic is 150 miles wide! It is, therefore, also sometimes called as the River Sea.

The Amazon originates in a glacier stream in the Peruvian Andes Mountains. The river got its name from the Spanish explorers who first discovered the river. Female warriors called 'Icamiabas', which means 'women without husbands' attacked Francisco Orellana and his party as they searched for cinnamon trees. After the battle, Orellana named the river 'Rio Amazonas' after these warrior women he fought. He compared these women to the Amazons of ancient Greek mythology.

The Amazon River basin is home to many varied plants and animals. More than 1/3 of the known plant species are found in the Amazon

Rainforest. More than 5,600 species of fish live in the Amazon River and more are being discovered each day. The Amazon River is also home to many mammals. Some well-known creatures found here are the Amazon River dolphin, catfish, giant otter and the most ferocious fish in the world, piranha. But perhaps the most famous inhabitant of the Amazon River is the heaviest snake in the world, Anaconda. Do you know that most of the species found in the Amazon Basin are found nowhere else in the world!

The Amazon River has the most number of tributaries as compared to any other river in the world. It has about 1500 tributaries and among them 17 are more than 930 miles long.

A few cities are also part of the Amazon Basin. The largest city in the Amazon River is Manaus which is located in Brazil. As people manage to live in only a few areas along the Amazon River, the river is also used as a means of transport. Do you know that there are no bridges on the Amazon River! It is because for most of its length, this massive river flows through the Amazon Rainforest. Interestingly, the Amazon Rainforest is also called the lungs of the world.

It is, therefore, correct to say that the mighty Amazon River stands out among the other rivers of the world.

 **Complete the sentences**

Read the sentences given below and complete them with the help of the chapter.

1. The Amazon pours ....

    the Atlantic Ocean per second!

2. The Amazon has the combined waters of ....

    ....

3. Some of the creatures found in the Amazon are ....
   ....

4. Amazon has many tributaries. Some of them ....
   ....

5. The river is used as a means of transport because ....
   ....

✓ Pick the correct answer

Choose the correct answers from the multiple choices given.

1. The Amazon is the biggest river in terms of ....
   a. Its length
   b. The water it contains
   c. Its size

2. The Amazon is also called ....
   a. River Sea
   b. Sea
   c. Living River

3. The heaviest snake in the world is called ....
   a. Python
   b. Anaconda
   c. Rattle Snake

4. The Amazon Basin is called ....

   a. The heart of the Amazon

   b. The lungs of the world

   c. The lungs of South America

Word ladder

Let's make a word ladder. You can change one letter at each step and make a new word. All the words that you make should be of four letters only. Go on then, reach from *Tree* to *Sail*.

TREE

B _ _ _

_ _ _ T

_ _ I _

F _ _ _

_ _ _ L

SAIL

Words and their meanings

Read the words given below. With the help of a dictionary find out their meanings and write in the table.

Words	Meanings
Boast	
Hollow	
Terrible	
Devour	
Budge	
Gigantic	

Know the rivers!

Write a short note on the world's longest river, Nile.

....

....

....

....

....

....

Punctuation

Read the following sentences. Use the capital letters, commas and full stops in these sentences wherever required. Then write the sentences in the space provided.

1. my aunt sally bought me a skateboard

   My aunt Sally bought me a skateboard.

2. father won a trip to spain portugal and france

   Father won a trip to Spain, Portugal and France.

3. sam bought a new camera and a tripod

   Sam bought a new camera and a tripod.

4. my sister rita went camping in august

   My sister Rita went camping in August.

5. the flowers bloom during the spring season

   The flowers bloom during the spring season.

6. mia, tara and betty went to watch a movie

   Mia, Tara and Betty went to watch a movie.

7. when it rains pauline goes to the attic to hide herself from the rains

   When it rains, Pauline goes to the attic to hide herself from the rains.

8. the hurricane brought rains water winds and landslides

   The hurricane brought rains, water, winds and landslides.

Fun to Know

A warming up discussion
- What is a pirate?
- Suppose you have found a great treasure. Where will you keep it?

Treasure Island

My father ran the Admiral Benbow inn. One day, an unkempt old seaman, with a deep white slash across his cheek came to the inn, lugging his sea-chest along. Whistling to himself, he sang an old sea-song:

'Fifteen men on the dead man's chest—Yo-ho-ho and a bottle of rum!'

'I'll stay here a bit,' he told my father. 'I'm a plain man; I only want rum, bacon and eggs and watch the ships at sea. Call me Captain.'

Throwing down a few gold pieces on my father's desk, he commanded him to tell him when it would be finished. He appeared like someone who was obeyed.

He was a very silent man by custom. All day he hung round the cove or upon the cliffs with a brass telescope; all evening he sat in a corner of the parlour next to the fire and drank rum. Every day when he came back from his stroll he would ask if any seafaring men had gone by along the road.

His stay at our inn from a few days turned to weeks and then for months. Also, all his money was exhausted but my father never asked him for more. As winters came, my father's health worsened. So my mother and I began to look after the inn. One January morning, I was setting the breakfast table when a pale man came in.

'Come here, lad, is this table for my mate, Bill?' he asked.

I learnt that the Captain had a name, Billy Bones. I told him he was out walking. He dragged me behind the parlour door and said that we would wait for him here. At last the Captain came in and walked straight to his breakfast table.

'Bill!' called out the stranger loudly.

As the Captain saw him, all colour drained out of his face. He gasped, 'Black Dog!'

Then, I left the parlour. But soon, I heard loud voices coming from there. Minutes later, the stranger ran out. I went to the Captain and saw him crashed on the floor breathing loudly and hard. Just then, Doctor Livesey came in to see my father.

The Captain had had a stroke. We took him to his room. Dr Livesey said that he needed a week's rest. And that another stroke would take his life. When the captain learnt that he would have to rest for a week, he was terrified. He cried, 'They will have the black spot on me by then. That man was bad but there are worse than him. It's my old sea-chest they're after.'

I was confused. The next day, my father passed away. The day after the funeral, as I stood at the inn's door, I saw a blind man, trudging along the road. He looked dreadful, was hunched and wore a tattered sea-cloak with a hood and wore green shades over his eyes. He inquired if it was Admiral Benbow Inn. I said it was and led him inside.

'Now, boy,' he said coldly, 'take me in to the Captain or I'll break your arm.'

I had never heard a voice so cruel, cold and ugly and I obeyed him at once.

I opened the parlour door, and cried, 'Here's a friend for you, Bill.'

The poor Captain raised his eyes, and the colour drained from his face.

'Boy, take his left hand by the wrist and bring it near to my right,' he said. As I did so, he passed something into the Captain's hand. Then, without another word, he went out of the inn. When he left, the Captain looked at his palm and cried, 'Ten o'clock! Six hours!' He sprang to his feet. But immediately, he fell on his face upon the floor. I ran to him calling to my mother. But he was already dead.

When my mother came, I lost no time in telling her all that I knew. We were now uncertain if we were safe at the inn. We went to the village downhill but no one came to help us. So we returned to our inn, bolting the door behind us. 'Now, Jim, get the key around the captain's neck,' said my mother.

With the key, we opened the Captain's chest. Among many other things including clothes, pistols, a telescope, tobacco, money, some of which my mother took for the amount he owned us, we also found a bundle tied in an oilcloth. I took it with me.

We were closing the chest when I heard the tap-tapping of the blind man's stick upon the frozen road. He came and struck it sharp on the inn door. We heard the handle being turned and the bolt rattling as he tried to enter. Then it ceased. He went back. Knowing that trouble was near, we decided to go to the village. We were barely outside when we saw pirates along with the blind man hurrying to our inn. Quickly, I hid us under a little bridge. From there, we could hear everything.

Curious, I crept back to the inn to see what was happening. I saw seven or eight men and the blind man in front of our inn. A few went inside and found Bill dead.

'Search him for the key,' cried the blind man. But they did not find what they were looking for. 'Search for the boy!' he cried. But before they could do so, I heard a loud whistle. It was a signal to warn them of the approaching danger.

Then, there was a tramp of horses galloping. Just then, a pistol-shot was heard from the hedge side. The pirates turned at once and ran. The blind man ran with them but he walked straight into the approaching horses and got trampled under the horses' hooves, though the rider tried to avoid him. As the rider checked the dead man, I sprang out and requested him to take me and my mother to the village.

Then, while my mother was being looked after, for she was in a bad state, I went to meet Dr Livesey. I found him sitting with Squire Trelawney in the library. In no time I had told them all that had happened since the arrival of Billy Bones. They sat silent a while until the doctor addressed me.

'And so, Jim,' said the Doctor, 'do you have the oilskin packet?'

The Doctor carefully opened the seals and there fell out the map of an island with latitude and longitude, surroundings, names of hills and bays and inlets. There was a hill in the centre, marked 'The Spy-glass.' Along with this there were some crosses marked on the map. It was a treasure map!

In no time, it was decided to go on this treasure hunt. After quite an adventure, we did manage to get the treasure and now we are living comfortably and it is only us who knows where the remaining treasure is kept still.

 **Let's remember the story**

Answer the following questions.

1. Who was Billy Bones?

2. When did the captain have a heart attack?

3. Who next came to meet the captain at the inn?

4. What did they find in the captain's chest?

5. What happened to the blind man?

6. What did the Treasure Map look like?

 **Words and their meanings**

Read the words given below. With the help of a dictionary find out their meanings and write in the table.

Words	Meanings
Stroll	
Uneasy	
Trudge	
Futile	
Tramp	
Gallop	

 **A wannabe pirate!**

If you could be a pirate, what kind of a pirate would you like to be? Write a few lines about the pirate that you would be.

....

....

....

....

....
....

Prefixes and suffixes

Given below are a few prefixes and suffixes along with a number of words. Use them together to make new words.

non-	ex-	de-	-less	-ness	-able
sense	hale	flate	change	fiction	existent	clude
ceed	void	mean	code	crease		

....

....

....

....

 Let's hear your thoughts

What kind of a boy is Jim Hawkins? Which of his qualities come out from the given passage?

....

....

....

....

51

Fun to Know

A warming up discussion
- Did you have a strange adventure?
- What did you feel during that time?

Alice in Wonderland

One day, Alice was sitting on a river bank with her sister, when a White Rabbit ran past her. 'I'm late,' said the Rabbit. Startled by the Rabbit's remark, Alice followed him down a rabbit hole. The moment Alice entered the rabbit hole, she fell down into a deep well.

Alice was surprised as the walls of the well were covered with cupboards and shelves that contained all sorts of things. As Alice continued to fall, she thought, 'I hope I don't come out from the other side of the earth.' She fell down for a long time until she fell on soft earth, unhurt. As she got up, she saw the White Rabbit turning a corner and quickly followed him. Soon, she reached a big hall with many doors. But the White Rabbit was nowhere to be seen.

'Where am I?' said Alice as she looked around herself. In the middle of the hall, she saw a three-legged glass table on which a tiny golden key was kept. She tried the key into the keyhole of every door but couldn't open any. Just then, she saw a small door. She tried the key in the keyhole of the small door and to her surprise, it opened! Beyond the door, she saw a beautiful garden. 'How can I go to that garden?' Alice muttered.

Just when Alice was wondering how to reach the garden, she saw a bottle labelled 'DRINK ME' kept on the glass table. Alice drank the contents of the bottle and instantly began shrinking. She was barely a few inches tall, when Alice realised that the key was left on the glass table, which was now too high for her. Just then, Alice saw a cake, labelled 'EAT ME', kept under the table.

Alice ate the cake and magically became nine feet tall. Frightened by her height, she started crying. Soon, a pool of tears had formed at her feet. Just then, the White Rabbit returned. 'Goodness Gracious!' said the White Rabbit seeing her and quickly scuttled away leaving his gloves and a fan behind. When he had left, Alice picked up the fan and began fanning herself. A few minutes later, she realised that she was shrinking and it was because of the fan. When she was her right size, she stopped fanning herself and dropped the fan.

The next moment, Alice fell into the pool made of her own tears. She started swimming and met various birds and animals. Together with many arguments and disapprovals, the animals along with Alice started swimming towards the shore. Finally, they all reached the land. They were all dripping wet when a Dodo said, 'Let us run a Caucus Race.' With a cheer everyone agreed. The next minute, all the animals and Alice started running in a haphazard manner. Half an hour later, the Dodo shouted, 'STOP!' Everyone stopped running and to their surprise, everyone was dry.

The race was finished and all the animals went to their homes. Alice was once again left alone. But just then the White Rabbit returned. Seeing Alice, he said, 'Mary Ann, go home and fetch my gloves and a fan!' Alice was surprised but she understood that the White Rabbit had mistaken  her for his maid. She at once, went towards the house of the White Rabbit and soon found it.

Alice went inside and soon found a drawer full of gloves and took out a pair and then also picked up a fan and made to go out of the house. Suddenly, she saw a bottle labelled 'DRINK ME.' 'I wonder what will happen now,' said Alice and drank the contents of the bottle in a jiffy.

And the next moment, Alice started growing. She grew and she grew! In no time, her hands and feet were sticking out of the windows and her head was sticking to the ground. 'Oh dear! What will I do now?' cried Alice. A few minutes had gone by when there was a knock on the door. But the door wouldn't open!

'Open the door Mary Ann,' shouted the White Rabbit impatient. Suddenly, he screamed, 'A monster inside my house!' He had seen her hands sticking out of the windows of her house.

Soon, a few animals gathered around the house to help the White Rabbit bring out the monster. And they began to throw stones at the windows. Alice grabbed them and started eating them for the stones had changed to cakes! 'I hope I shall change,' said Alice as she ate a cake.

Can you guess what would have happened to Alice when she had eaten the cake? Well, she became small once again and ran out of the White Rabbit's house. But that was not the end. She had many more adventures and strange experiences in Wonderland. Wouldn't it be better if you read about those adventures on your own!

Let's remember the story

Answer the following questions.

1. What was lined along the walls of the well?
2. What did Alice see beyond the little door?
3. How did Alice become small?
4. How did Alice dry herself?
5. What did the White Rabbit ask Alice to bring?
6. How did Alice become large in the White Rabbit's house?

Pick the correct answer

Choose the correct answers from the multiple choices given.

1. Alice went after the White Rabbit as ....
   a. She had heard him sing
   b. She had heard him speak
   c. It was her favourite rabbit

2. Alice fell into a pool of ....
   a. Tears
   b. Candies
   c. Water

3. Alice and the other animals got dry when they ran ....
   a. The Caucus Race
   b. The Evening Race
   c. The Flamingo Race

4. The White Rabbit threw .... to bring out the monster in his house.

    a. Leaves

    b. Pancakes

    c. Stones

 Punctuation

Read the following sentences given below. Use the capital letters, commas and full stops in these sentences wherever required. Then write the sentences in the space provided.

1. orange green blue and pink are my favourite colours

2. keep a look out while walking on the road

3. sam was unable to see through the thick fog

4. mrs smith's cat is black and white in colour

5. friday saturday and sunday are my favourite days

6. i will be 14 years old in august

7. my sister agnes likes to play basketball

8. i went to san francisco to see the golden gate bridge

 Idioms

Match the idioms given in Column A with their meanings in Column B.

Idioms	Meanings
At the drop of a hat	A useless rock that looks like gold
Dog days	To go to sleep
Fool's gold	To stay happy even in a tough situation
Hit the hay	Willing to do something at once
Keep your chin up	Someone who is new to the area or a place
New kid on the block	Hottest days of summer season

Word Grid

Find the given words in the word grid given below.

Alice	White Rabbit	Caucus Race	Mary Ann
Cake	Wonderland	Tears	

M	W	O	N	D	E	R	L	A	N	D	P
A	W	H	I	T	E	R	A	B	B	I	T
R	U	W	R	A	U	E	L	H	S	D	E
Y	A	E	D	S	E	D	I	D	K	O	A
A	N	U	S	T	E	N	C	A	K	E	R
N	K	N	A	U	R	L	E	E	O	I	S
N	C	A	U	C	U	S	R	A	C	E	L
R	A	S	O	C	D	E	T	H	K	W	T

57

Fun to Know

A warming up discussion
- Do you have a pet?
- Have you travelled with your pet anywhere?

The Owl and the Pussy-Cat

The Owl and the Pussy-Cat went to sea

In a beautiful pea-green boat:

They took some honey, and plenty of money

Wrapped up in a five-pound note.

The Owl looked up to the stars above,

And sang to a small guitar,
'O lovely Pussy, O Pussy, my love,
What a beautiful Pussy you are,
You are,
You are!
What a beautiful Pussy you are!'

Pussy said to the Owl, 'You elegant fowl,
How charmingly sweet you sing!
Oh! let us be married; too long we have tarried,
But what shall we do for a ring?'
They sailed away, for a year and a day,
To the land where the bong-tree grows;
And there in a wood a Piggy-wig stood,
With a ring at the end of his nose,
His nose,
His nose,
With a ring at the end of his nose.

'Dear Pig, are you willing to sell for one shilling
Your ring?' Said the Piggy, 'I will.'
So they took it away, and were married next day
By the turkey who lives on the hill.
They dined on mince and slices of quince,
Which they ate with a runcible spoon;

And hand in hand, on the edge of the sand,

They danced by the light of the moon,

The moon,

The moon,

They danced by the light of the moon.

(Edward Lear)

 **Complete the sentences**

Read the sentences given below and complete them with the help of the poem.

1. The Owl and the Pussy Cat went to the sea ....
   ....

2. After listening to the Owl's song, the Pussy Cat said ....
   ....

3. They sailed to the land ....
   ....

4. They asked the pig to give them ....
   ....

5. Owl and the Pussy Cat were married by ....
   ....

6. After their wedding, they danced ....
   ....

Antonyms

Can you match the words and their antonyms given in the following table?

Words	Antonyms
Plenty	Crude
Elegant	Finish
charming	Bottom
Tarry	Shortage
Wrap	offensive
Edge	Unwrap

 Pick the correct answer

Choose the correct answers from the multiple choices given.

1. The Owl and the Pussy cat were in a....................
   a. Pea-green boat
   b. A sailboat
   c. A car

2. The Owl played a....................
   a. Harp
   b. Guitar
   c. Xylophone

61

3. The pig had a ring around his.................

   a. Nose

   b. Finger

   c. Ear

4. The Owl and the Pussy Cat were married by a........................

   a. Lark

   b. Turkey

   c. Ostrich

Practise writing sentences

Use the following words in your own sentences.

1. Beautiful

   ....

2. Star

   ....

3. Moon

   ....

4. Hill

   ....

5. Sand

   ....

6. Wood

   ....

# A budding writer!

You have read the above poem. What do you think of this poem? Tell us your views.

Fun to Know

A warming up discussion
- Who carves things out of stone or wood?
- Have you ever seen them working?

Stone Flower

A long time ago, in a small village in the Ural Mountains, there lived a craftsman called Prokopyich. He was renowned throughout the Urals for the crafts he made out of malachite and was the finest gem carver. He taught boys from around the Urals his craft but none of them were talented enough.

In the village where Prokopyich lived, there was an orphan boy called Danila. A kind old woman looked after him. The woman taught him the lore of plants, and one day told him about the Stone Flower that was on the Malachite Mountain. She told him it was the most beautiful flower in the world. But she also warned him, 'Whoever finds that flower will never be happy.'

Soon, Danila too went to Prokopyich to study gem carving. He was surprisingly gifted. Prokopyich loved the boy as if he were his own son. Several years passed and Danila grew up. One day, the king sent Danila a commission to make a vase from malachite along with a sketch of what he wanted. Danila began the intricate task but he was unsatisfied with the idea of the sketch. Every day he went to the

woods looking for inspiration and to make the vase better. At last, he finished making the task but he was not happy with what he had made though everyone greatly praised him. But Danila said, 'The vase lacks living beauty.'

One very old craftsman warned him, 'Don't even think that way. Otherwise you would become a servant of the Mistress of Copper Mountain. Her workers live and work in the Copper Mountain and nobody ever sees them. Once I was lucky enough to see their work. Magnificent it was!'

Dissatisfied, Daniel began wandering the hills looking for the perfect piece of stone to make his craft. Worried about Danila, Prokopyich had him engaged to a wise and pretty girl called Katya hoping that he would forget about the Stone Flower. But it was not so. One day, in the hills, he heard a whisper saying, 'Danila-Craftsman, look for the stone on Serpent Hill.' He turned around and saw the dim outline of a woman, which vanished immediately. He understood that it was the Mistress of Copper Mountain! He did find a huge block of malachite on the Serpent Hill.

But he was disappointed by what he had made and said sadly, 'I want to see Stone Flower!' Meanwhile a day was fixed for the wedding of Danila and Katya. The day before the wedding he went for a walk to Serpent Hill again.

All a sudden the Mistress of Copper Mountain appeared before him. She said, 'I could show you my Stone Flower but afterwards you will regret it. Those who have seen my Flower have left their family and come to live in my mountain. Think about Prokopyich and Katya who love you.'

But Danila was determined to see the Stone Flower. So she showed him the wonderful Stone Flower. In the evening Danila came to the village. But in no time, he felt sad and returned to the Serpent Mountain. Three years passed by and no one knew where Danila had gone. In the meantime, Katya did not marry. She started earning her living by making stone brooches.

Often, she went to Serpent Hill hoping to find good pieces of stone. Soon, the brooches she made became greatly sought after. One day, when she came to the Serpent Hill, Katya remembered Danila and cried sorrowfully, 'Where are you, my beloved Danila?' After some time, when she calmed down, she realised that she was in an unfamiliar part of the woods. She wondered, 'Is this the magic mountain?'

As Katya looked around the hill cautiously, suddenly, it seemed to her that a man who looked like Danila stood near her looking at her. Happy, she ran towards Danila but it was just a shadow. She cried, 'Danila, where are you? Answer me!' Then suddenly the Mistress of Copper Mountain stood before her. She demanded, 'Why have you come here? If you want stones take them and go away.'

Brave Katya replied, 'I don't need your stones. Give me my Danila back.' Hearing this, the Mistress laughed. 'Do you know who I am?' Katya cried out, 'I do know who you are but I also know that Danila wants to return to me.' The Mistress said, 'All right, let him speak then.'

At once, Danila stood before them. The Mistress said, 'You have to choose, Danila.'

Danila sighed, 'I am sorry. I can't forget the people I love. I think about Katya all the time.' The Mistress smiled and said, 'All right, Danila. Go back home. And for your honesty, you shall remember what you have learnt here. Remember to tell others that you had gone to a faraway kingdom to improve your skills.'

Katya and Danila returned home joyfully. The villagers were surprised to see Danila. When asked where he had been, he lied. Soon, he married Katya and they lived happily. And as for his craft, he became the greatest carver in the Ural Mountains.

Let's remember the story

Answer the following questions.
1. What was the legend about the stone flower?
2. Why was Danila always unhappy?
3. Whom did Danila meet in the forest? What did she give him?
4. What happened the day before Danila and Katya were going to get married?
5. What did Katya say when she met the Mistress of the Copper Mountain?
6. What was the blessing of the Mistress of the Copper Mountain to Danila?

Words and their meanings

Read the words given below. With the help of a dictionary find out their meanings and write in the table.

Words	Meanings
Commission	
Whisper	
Carve	
Regret	
Wonderful	
Cautious	

# Think and fill

Read the following sentences. Fill in the blanks using the correct articles, *a*, *an*, and *the*.

1. .... dog attacked me and ran away.
2. I am to meet him .... hour from now.
3. Martha is wearing .... colourful dress.
4. Joe needs .... glass of juice.
5. They are planning a trek along .... Alps.
6. Lisa is going to dress like .... witch at Halloween.
7. They found themselves in .... unusual situation.
8. He is eating .... apple and .... mango followed by .... glass of milk.

# Circling the words

Read the passage given below carefully and put a circle around the adjectives.

It was like any other country village. But in this village people had strange beliefs. One among them was regarding the haunted house just outside the village where an old, bad tempered man lived. Often people heard sharp, squeaky sounds from his house in the evening. It was when people said that two ghosts came to his house.

The old man refused to leave his house. 'That is all that I have left,' he said when people asked him to come and live comfortably in another house in the village.

Each day, the old man took his two healthy goats to the green pasture to let them graze. He carried his wooden stick along. Everyone wondered how he could stand the terrifying ghosts in his house.

Fun to Know

A warming up discussion
- Which are the most beautiful birds you have seen?
- Can you name one bird that has beautiful plumes?

Birds of Paradise

We see birds all around us. They have varied sizes, colours and plumes. They even live in varied habitats and they have different food patterns. Among the birds that you have seen, which do you think is the most beautiful bird? Your answers would be varied but you must have heard about the Birds of Paradise.

The Birds of Paradise are some of the most strikingly beautiful birds found on earth. They are distinguished by their striking colours and bright plumage of yellow, blue, scarlet, red and green. The bright colours of these birds make them stand out among the other attractive birds of the bird kingdom. These birds are found in the misty rainforests of New Guinea. Some species, however, are also found in Australia. These birds belong to the family *Paradisaeidae* and there are more than three dozens species in this family.

The males of the species have vibrant feathered ruffs or amazingly elongated feathers, which are known as wires or streamers. And besides these adornments, some species even have enormous head plumes, breast shields and head fans. No other bird except the Birds of Paradise has such distinctive ornaments. Do you know that these birds also lend their name to a South African flower! It is believed that this flower resembles the birds of paradise in flight.

The males of the species display their beautiful array of feathers, plumes and streamers during courtship. Their elaborate plumage is to attract the attention of the female. But that is not all. They even venture in to long and complicated dances. Theses dances and poses can go from a few minutes to a few hours. If one gets a chance to see their elaborate dances, it is phenomenal. Do you know that the Birds of Paradise are crow-like in terms of their body structure? These birds are indeed related to the crows and jays.

The females of these species are ordinary looking compared to the males. The females are usually brown in colour and their plumage usually helps them to blend in with their surroundings. These birds have long bills and strong claws. They are solitary birds and it is only during the courtship period that they come together. But it is the attractive plumage of these birds that has put them in danger. The elaborate plumes and adorations also make them the target of skin hunters. As a result, some species of these beautiful birds were brought to the point of extinction.

Though the natives living in Papua New Guinea have used the plumes of these birds for thousands of years, to the western world these incredible birds became known only in 1996. It was then that David Attenborough had shown the footage of these birds to the west and stunned them. The natives have used the plumes and feathers of these birds to adorn themselves. It is for this purpose that they are hunted. But in recent years efforts have been put to protect these birds and conserve them in their unique habitat.

Let's remember the story

Answer the following questions.
1. Where are the Birds of Paradise found?
2. What are the striking features of the Birds of Paradise?
3. Name the distinctive ornaments of the males of these species.
4. What is the appearance of female Birds of Paradise?
5. Why are these birds hunted?
6. A South African flower is also named after them. Why?

Practise writing sentences

Use the following words in your own sentences.

1. Distinguish

   ....

2. Attractive

   ....

3. Strong

   ....

4. Together

   ....

5. Feathers

   ....

6. Adorn

   ....

 **Word ladder**

Let's make a word ladder. You can change **one letter** at each step and make a new word. All the words that you make should be of four letters only. Go on then, reach from **Bird** to **King**.

BIRD

_ A _ _

_ I _ _

_ _ N _

K _ _ _

KING

 **Crossword**

With the help of given clues, complete the crossword.

Across:
1. A place where the Birds of Paradise are found
2. The Birds of Paradise need to be conserved
3. These creatures fly in the sky

Down:
4. Birds bodies are covered with these
5. Birds of Paradise are related to these birds
6. These birds do this to impress the females

 ## Synonyms

Match the words with their synonyms given in the following table.

Words	Synonyms
Habitat	Mix
Attractive	Dying out
Elongated	Territory
Solitary	Long
Extinction	Good-looking
Blend	Alone

Fun to Know

A warming up discussion
- Do you know where England is?
- Do you know anything about King Arthur?

The Sword in the Stone

A long time ago, in Britain, the Saxons were causing a lot of trouble. Uther, the High-King of Britain fought valiantly to keep the Saxons at bay. While returning from one such battle, he saw Lady Igraine. He fell in love with her. And in no time, the two got married.

Some time later, the two were blessed with a son while they were staying in Tintagel Castle. They named their son Arthur. No sooner was the child born that Merlin, King Uther's advisor and a powerful magician, suggested that the child should be protected. 'The Saxons would try to harm the child,' said Merlin. King Uther agreed with Merlin and gave his newborn son to Merlin for the child's safety.

Clever Merlin sent Arthur to the countryside to the house of Sir Ector. He looked after the infant like his own son. Time passed, young Arthur grew up in the countryside with his foster brother, Kay. All this time, he did not know who his real parents were. Meanwhile, King Uther died and no one knew that he had a heir to the throne. So there were many nobles who fought among themselves to become the next High-King of Britain.

But Merlin knew about the rightful heir to the throne of

Britain. Then something miraculous happened for a large stone appeared in a busy square in London. A sword was stuck in that stone. When the people saw the stone and the sword they were astonished. A message was written on the sword. It read 'Whoever will pull the sword from the stone will be the rightful High-King of Britain.'

Merlin persuaded the people saying that it was a divine sign to find a just and powerful ruler. Many lords and local rulers tried to pull out the sword but no one was successful, though they tried a number of times.

Years passed by and yet there was no king in Britain though many nobles continued to fight each other to be the High-King of Britain. Meanwhile, Arthur, King Uther's son had turned fifteen years old. Once, Arthur along with his foster family went to London as Kay had to participate in a tournament. Once in London, Arthur realized that Kay had no sword with him. So, he went looking for a sword for Kay.

'Ah! A sword!' he said seeing the sword in the stone in the square. He rushed towards the stone and pulled out the sword like one pulls out knife from amidst butter.

Those who saw him pull out the sword were transfixed. Meanwhile, Arthur went and gave the sword to Kay. Kay knew about the sword in the stone. When he noticed the message on the sword, he asked, 'Arthur, how did you get this sword?' Quickly, Arthur told him everything.

But no one believed that Arthur had pulled out the sword from the stone. So Arthur took them to the stone in the square, placed the sword in the stone and pulled it out a number of times. Everyone was amazed. Soon, Merlin too came to the square. Merlin knew that the boy was King Uther's son when Arthur pulled out the sword in front of Merlin.

Days later, Arthur was crowned King by St. Dubricius. The people were joyous.

However, eleven local kings did not accept young Arthur as the High-King. So, they joined hands and started a rebellion against the newly crowned king.

Merlin then decided to help young King Arthur to defeat the eleven local rulers. Merlin took him to a lake. In that lake lived the 'Lady of the Lake'. When they reached the middle of the lake, a hand came out of the water holding a sword in a scabbard. 'Take the sword, Arthur,' Merlin said. When they came ashore, Merlin said, 'This sword is called Excalibur. Its scabbard is magical. If you use Excalibur in a fight, you would always defeat your opponent. If you keep the scabbard with you, you would not get hurt.'

So Arthur with his magical sword managed to defeat the eleven rebel kings. They accepted him as their High-King.

After his victory, Arthur set up his Royal palace at Camelot. Few years passed by and Arthur got married to a fair lady called Guinevere. She was the daughter of King Leodegrance of Cameliard. As a wedding present, King Leodegrance gave King Arthur a large round table. With time, many knights joined as soldiers for King Arthur. The bravest of these knights were allowed to sit with King Arthur at the round table. These chosen knights were known as the 'Knights of the Round Table'.

Under the reign of King Arthur and his brave knights, there was peace all over Britain.

Let's remember the story

Answer the following questions.

1. Who were the parents of King Arthur?
2. What precaution did Merlin took to protect young Arthur?
3. What was written on the sword in the stone?
4. When did Arthur pull out the sword from the stone?
5. How did Merlin help young Arthur defeat the eleven local rulers?
6. What do you mean by the term 'Knights of the Round Table'?

Pick the correct answer

Choose the correct answers from the multiple choices given.

1. Merlin was a powerful...............
   a. Wrestler
   b. Magician
   c. Juggler

2. What appeared in the middle of a busy street?
   a. A stone with a sword in it
   b. A troupe of jugglers
   c. A group of kings

3. Merlin took Arthur to the......................................
   a. A good king
   b. Lady of the Lake
   c. A powerful sorcerer

4. King Arthur lived in.........................

    a. London

    b. Cambridge

    c. Camelot

 **Word ladder**

Let's make a word ladder. You can change one letter at each step and make a new word. All the words that you make should be of four letters only. Go on then, reach from Heap to Real.

 **Prepositions**

Fill in the blanks using the preposition given below.

| for | since | on | by | under | after | around | off |

1. The children ran .... the ice cream van.
2. Frightened by the storm, Bozo hid himself .... the bed.
3. He has been practising football .... morning.
4. She turned .... the fan before going out of her room.
5. The children are standing .... the pool side waiting for their instructor.
6. The package is kept ...... the table.
7. The boys went .... the block looking for the lost dog.
8. Mother baked a cake .... Tom's birthday.

Prefixes and suffixes

Given below are a few prefixes and suffixes along with a number of words. Use them together to make new words.

-y	-est	-al	un-	dis-			
Mess	lucky	comic	anger	tear	bright	full	late
approve	dispose	brave	big	festive	classic	cream	fault

....

....

....

....

Fun to Know

A warming up discussion
- Have you ever helped anyone? How?
- Why should we help those in need?

The Four Dragons

Once upon a time, there were no rivers and lakes on earth but only the Eastern Sea, in which lived four dragons: the Long Dragon, the Yellow Dragon, the Black Dragon and the Pearl Dragon.

One day, the four dragons flew from the sea into the sky. They soared and dived, playing hide-and-seek in the clouds. 'Come over here quickly!' the Pearl Dragon cried out suddenly. 'What is it?' asked the other three, looking down in the direction where the Pearl Dragon pointed. On the earth they saw many people putting out fruits and cakes, and burning incense sticks as they prayed. Then, a white-haired woman, kneeling on the ground with a thin boy on her back, murmured, 'Please send rain quickly God of Heaven so that we can grow rice for our children to eat.'

They prayed so, as there had been no rain for a long time. The crops had withered, the grass had turned yellow and the fields cracked under the scorching sun. 'How poor the people are!' said the Yellow Dragon.

'They will die if it doesn't rain soon,' said the Long Dragon. Then he suggested, 'Let's go and beg the Jade Emperor to send rain on earth.'

Saying so, the Long Dragon leapt into the clouds. The others followed closely and flew towards the Heavenly Palace of the Jade Emperor.

Being in charge of all the affairs in heaven, on earth and in the sea, the Jade Emperor was very powerful. He was not pleased to see the dragons rushing in. 'Why did you come here instead of staying in the sea and behaving yourselves?' thundered the Jade Emperor.

The Long Dragon stepped forward, bowed and said, 'The crops on earth are withering and dying, Your Majesty. I beg you to send rain down quickly!'

'All right. You go back first and I'll send some rain down tomorrow,' said the Jade Emperor. But he had no intention of doing so. He just wanted to get rid of the dragons so he had only pretended to listen to them.

'Thank you for your generosity, Your Majesty,' said the four dragons and bowing once again went out of the Heavenly Palace of the Jade Emperor.

The four dragons looked forward to the coming rains. However, ten days had passed by and yet not a single drop of rain had fallen on the ground. The suffering of the people had increased. The animals started dying and the earth had become cracked.

Seeing the suffering on earth, the four dragons were very sad. They understood that the Jade Emperor had only tried to pacify them. He did not care about the people on earth. The four dragons then decided to relieve the people of their misery. But how could they do so!

Then, the Long Dragon had an idea. He said, 'There is plenty of water in the sea. Why don't we scoop it up and spray it over the land.'

'That is a good idea!' said the other three dragons.

'But if the Jade Emperor finds out about this, we shall be severely punished,' said the Long Dragon.

'I will do anything to save the people,' said the Yellow Dragon resolutely.

'Let us get to work then,' said the Black Dragon and the Pearl Dragon, agreeing with the Yellow Dragon.

The next moment, the four dragon flew down to the sea, scooped up water in their mouths, flew back to the sky, put the water in the clouds. In similar manner, they continued to fly back and forth. Soon, the clouds were filled and soon it was raining.

'It's raining! It's raining!' cheered the people as the sea water started to pour as rain. 'Our crops will be saved now!'

The people started to leap with joy as it continued to rain. In no time, the Jade Emperor learnt what the four dragons had been doing to help the people on earth. Furious, he thundered, 'How dare the four dragons bring rain on earth without my permission?'

At once, he sent his troops to arrest the four dragons and to be brought before him. Seeing the troops, the four dragons let themselves be arrested peacefully.

When the Jade Emperor saw them, he commanded the Mountain God, 'At once, get four mountains to be placed upon them so that they would never be able to escape. They must learn to obey orders.'

Obeying orders, the Mountain God quickly summoned four mountains. Then, the four dragons were pressed down beneath those mountains, one mountain for one dragon. Imprisoned as they were, the dragons never regretted their actions.

Still determined to help the people on earth, the dragons turned themselves into rivers that flowed past high mountains and deep valleys, crossing the land from the west to the east and finally emptying into the sea. It was in this manner that the four great rivers of China were formed.

These four rivers are— the Heilongjian in the far north, the Huanghe or the Yellow River in central China, the Yangtze or Long River farther south and the Zhujiang River in the far south.

 **Let's remember the story**

Answer the following questions.

1. Which were the four dragons?
2. What did they see from the sky?

3. To whom did they go asking for mercy?
4. How did the dragons tried to help the people?
5. How were they punished?
6. How were the four great rivers of China formed?

Words and their meanings

Read the words given below. With the help of a dictionary find out their meanings and write in the table.

Words	Meanings
Murmur	
Wither	
Severe	
Resolute	
Sustain	
Regret	

Phrases, here we come!

Read the sentences below carefully. Complete them with the help of the phrases given in the box.

| by the book | a big fish in a small pond | mind your P's and Q's |
| as cool as a cucumber | a little bird told me | bated breath |

1. The children waited with .... for the result to be announced.

2. .... that you have broken the jam jar.
3. Rita went .... while writing her exam.
4. Throughout the interrogation, the thief was ....
5. While talking to the principle ....
6. Sue felt like a .... in the college.

Think and fill

Fill in the sentences using the correct words.

| arrested   Jade   spray   suffering   transformed   intention |

1. The four dragons saw the people on earth ....
2. They went to the .... Emperor asking him to help the people.
3. The Jade Emperor had no .... of helping the people.
4. The four dragons thought to .... water on the land.
5. The four dragons were ....
6. The dragons .... themselves into rivers.

Know the rivers!

Now that you have read the story, find out the location of the four rivers in China. Write small paragraphs on any two of the mentioned rivers.

....
....
....
....

Fun to Know

A warming up discussion
- Who is an astronaut?
- How do astronauts travel?

Neil Armstrong

There have been people in our world who have thought of travelling beyond the earth. These brave men and women have put in a lot of hard work and efforts before they were able to travel to other heavenly bodies. Can you name the first person who had gone to the Moon? You probably know the answer and you are right it was Neil Armstrong.

Neil Alden Armstrong was born on August 5, 1930 in Wapakoneta, Ohio. His father Stephen Armstrong was an auditor for the Ohio state government. The family moved many times. He was two years old when his father took him to the National Air Show to show him as the planes raced at the Cleveland Airport. From the moment Neil saw the planes, he loved them.

One morning in July 1936, his father told him about Ford Tri Motor, a new plane that was coming to the airport around noon. At once, Neil bombarded his father with his questions about the plane and his father was happy to answer them. Soon, they were dressed to go and watch the plane. But they not only watched the plane but also took a ride in it. Young Neil never forgot his first flight. Perhaps, it was from that moment that Neil had decided to become a pilot. While he was at school, Neil also took flying lessons at the airport. It was, therefore, no surprise that he had his pilot's license by the age of 15 years.

After completing school, Armstrong went to Purdue University from where he earned his bachelor's degree in aerospace engineering. He later went on to earn his masters degree at the University of Southern California. While he was in college, Neil was called up by the Navy and after flight training, he became a fully qualified Naval Aviator. It was also during this time that he fought in the Korean War where he had to fly fighters from aircraft carriers. Once during his flight, his plane was hit by the enemy but he was safely rescued.

After completing his college, Armstrong became a test pilot. As a test pilot, he flew various kinds of planes some of which were for experimental purposes. As a test pilot, he flew about 200 different kinds of aircrafts. In 1958, he was selected for U.S. Air Force's Man in Space Soonest Program. Neil was chosen for the program. Later, he was part of NASA Astronaut Corps. Along with some others, Neil went through a series of harsh physical tests. He passed these tests.

Armstrong first travelled into space aboard the Gemini 8. He was the command pilot of the spaceship and piloted the first successful docking of two vehicles in space. However, the mission was shortened. What Neil Armstrong did next made him world famous. On December 23, 1968 Neil was offered the command of Apollo 11. This was to be the first manned aircraft to land on the Moon. During this time, a race was underway between the United States and the Soviet Union to send a man to the moon. Both countries wanted to be the first to do so.

After months of practice and preparation, the Apollo 11 spacecraft was launched from Kennedy Space Center in Florida on July 16, 1969. Everyone was excited and prayed that the flight landed safely on the Moon. The landing was a success and Neil Armstrong immediately transmitted back, 'Houston, Tranquility Base here. The Eagle has landed.' A great cheer arose hearing these words. Do you know that Neil took his Eagle Scouts Badge to the Moon!

Few minutes after landing, Neil Armstrong went out of the spacecraft and took the first step on the Moon. This historic event took place on July 21, 1969. Neil famously said after his walk, 'That's one small step for man, one giant leap for mankind'. The three astronauts stayed on the Moon for 21 hours and collected rock samples. The three astronauts returned to Earth on July 24, as heroes. They were awarded the Presidential Medal of Freedom, the highest honour to be earned by a civilian from the US government.

After his spaceflight aboard Apollo 11, Neil Armstrong held many positions with NASA. He also worked as a professor of aerospace engineering at the University of Cincinnati. He died on August 25, 2012.

Let's remember the story

Answer the following questions.
1. When did Neil Armstrong first see planes?
2. When did Neil Armstrong decide to become a pilot?
3. What were his experiences as a Naval Aviator?
4. When did Neil Armstrong first travel into the space?
5. What famous words had Neil said from the Moon?
6. Which highest honour did he earn?

Punctuation

Read the following sentences given below. Use the capital letters, commas and full stops in these sentences wherever required. Then write the sentences in the space provided.

1. she lost her keys her wallet and her cell phone
   ....
2. sandra went to buy a puppy from the pet store
   ....
3. sam neil and andy are making a sand castle
   ....
4. athens is the capital of Greece
   ....
5. portugal is a part of the european continent
   ....
6. chris and suzy are playing in the park
   ....
7. my dog bozzo likes to eat ice cream
   ....
8. ben lily sue and bert are planting roses in the garden
   ....

Find friends

You are familiar with similar sounding words called rhyming words. Read the words in Column A and match them with similar sounding words in Column B.

Column A	Column B
Plane	Place
Show	Rest
Flight	Main
Rock	Knight
Space	Dock
Test	Mow

Widen your horizon

Find out about NASA. What does this organization do and what is it all about? Write what you have found out about NASA in the space provided below.

....
....
....
....
....

Be an astronaut!

Suppose you have become an astronaut. As an astronaut which planet would you like to fly to and why?

....
....
....
....
....

Fun to Know

A warming up discussion
- Do you lie to your friends?
- Have you ever told a lie to test someone?

The Honest Merchant

Characters

Merchant 1

Merchant 2

Girl

Grandmother

Narrator

Script

Narrator: Once, in a small town, two merchants took turns to sell their wares. They sold plates, pans, brooms, small articles of jewellery and even clothes. One day...

Merchant 1: I have all the things that you will need. Come and buy good quality goods.

Girl: Grandmother, look! What a beautiful bracelet that is! Can we buy it?

Grandmother: Of course, we can, my dear. Merchant, what is the price of the bracelet the girl wants?

Narrator: Now, the girl and her grandmother were poor. Seeing them, the merchant was hesitant to give them the bracelet.

Merchant 1: What can you pay for the bracelet?

Grandmother: We do not have money to pay for it. But you can have an old plate that we have,

Merchant 1: Let me see it.

Narrator: The plate was black. Seeing it, the merchant scratched it and saw that the plate was actually a silver plate. And then he thought of cheating the old woman.

Merchant 1: I am sorry but I cannot trade the bracelet for this plate. This plate is worth nothing to me.

Narrator: As he went away, the merchant had decided to come tomorrow and by some means have that plate. In the evening, the second merchant came to sell his wares. He too had the same bracelet which the girl saw and asked his grandmother to inquire if this merchant would sell her the bracelet.

Grandmother: My granddaughter wants a bracelet that you have. I have no money to give you in exchange for this bracelet. But I have a plate which I can give you. Here, look at it.

Merchant 2: Old lady, this plate is made of silver. All that I have is not enough to pay you for this plate.

Grandmother: But I have nothing else to give you.

Merchant 2: In that case, you can have all of my wares and you can also keep the 1000 coins that I have.

Grandmother: Oh! Thank you for your kindness.

Narrator: The second merchant sold the plate and made a good profit on it. He opened a small shop that sold cloth with the money he got. When the other merchant learnt how the fortunes of the other had turned, he was sorry for being greedy. He then changed his ways and began to lead an honest life.

Let's remember the story

Answer the following questions.

1. What did the two merchants sell?
2. What did the grandmother offered in exchange of the bracelet?
3. Why did the first merchant refuse to sell the bracelet?
4. Was the plate really just an ordinary plate?
5. What did the second merchant say when he saw the plate?
6. Why was the first merchant sorry?

Match the idioms given in Column A with their meanings in Column B.

Idioms	Meanings
An arm and a leg	To be very sick
Chow down	To have something secured
In the bag	For certain
No dice	Something which is very expensive
Sick as a dog	To eat
Without a doubt	To disagree

93

Word Grid

Find the given words in the grid below.

grandmother	merchant	bracelet	profit	plate	wares

R	B	T	E	A	I	H	O	N	M	P
G	R	A	N	D	M	O	T	H	E	R
W	A	H	I	I	A	N	W	P	R	O
O	C	P	T	C	H	E	A	T	C	F
T	E	W	W	T	W	S	R	I	H	I
P	L	A	T	E	R	T	I	G	A	T
R	E	R	R	A	T	Y	A	N	N	P
R	T	E	S	R	A	O	N	R	T	P
S	A	S	P	S	O	F	T	I	O	I

Let's perform!

Enact a small play in your class with the help of your teacher. The teacher can distribute the characters based on the story 'Wolf and the seven little kids' among the children. Have fun!

Dialogue writing

Write a short dialogue between you and your parents. Your teacher has asked you to gather all your old toys, clothes and books too. These objects will be distributed to needy children. The best dialogues can be enacted in the class.

Fun to Know

A warming up discussion
- What is a mystery?
- Do you know what Bermuda Triangle is?

The Bermuda Triangle

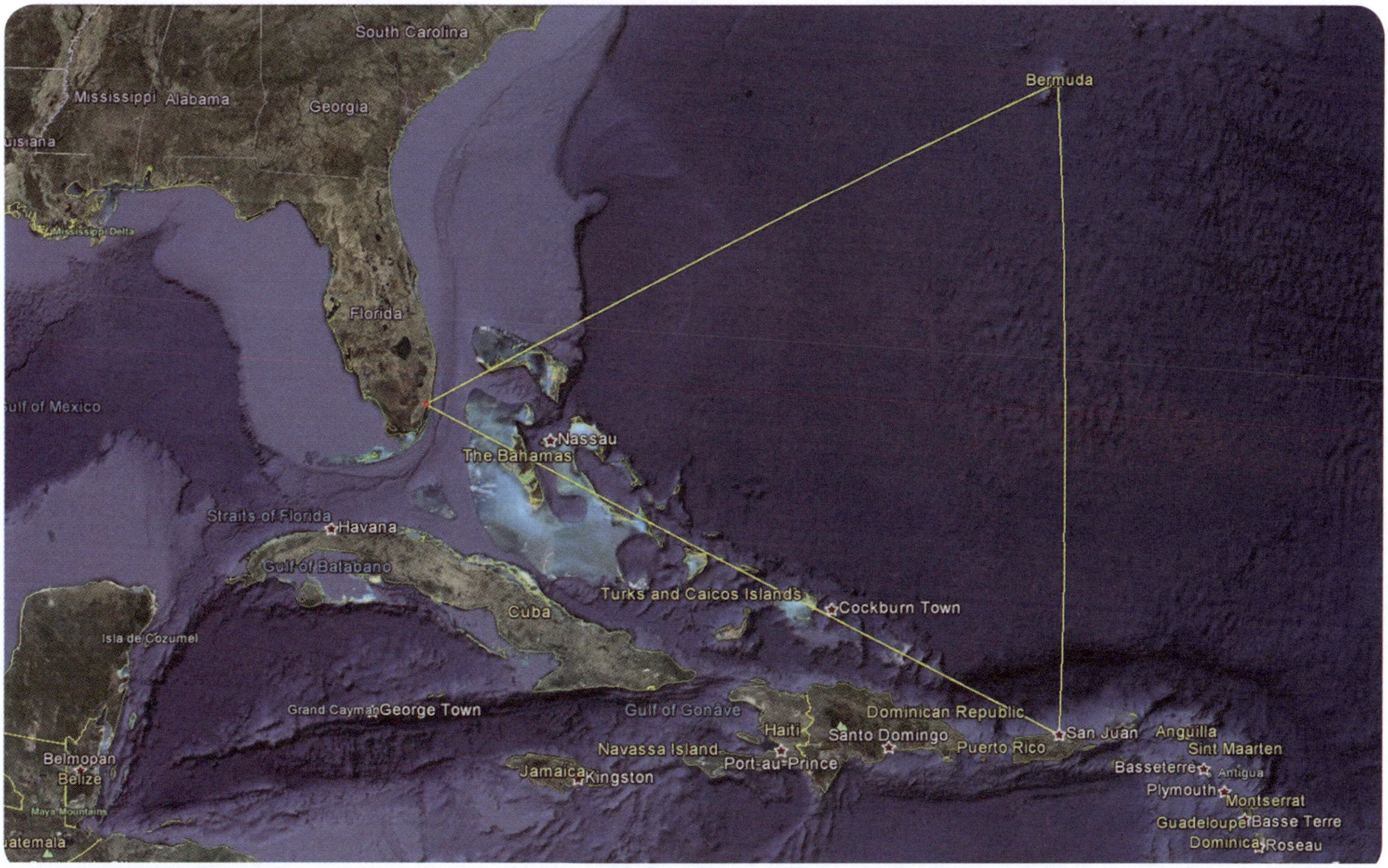

There are many mysterious happenings and structures in our world. Over the years there have been attempts to solve the reason behind them but no one had been successful so far. Anything mysterious awakens our curiosity and we make an attempt to solve the secret behind the unexplained. Sometimes or the other, you too would have tried to solve a secret. Perhaps you were successful in solving it or perhaps you only got more puzzled.

The mystery of the Bermuda Triangle is one among the unsolved mysteries of the world. The term Bermuda Triangle was first coined in a magazine in 1964. The Bermuda Triangle is a mysterious area in the North Atlantic Ocean. It is an area where ships and aircrafts have disappeared suddenly without any reason. And even their remains have not been found. It is also called the Devil's Triangle. The triangle is roughly thought to be defined by the vertices at Bermuda, San Juan in Puerto Rico and Miami, Florida. However, the US Navy does not recognize such a place or name.

This mysterious area was first noted in 1950 by E.V.W. Jones when he studied the recent ship losses in an Associated Press article. In 1952, the area was again mentioned in an article of the Fate magazine written by George Sand. However, the term Bermuda Triangle became popular when Vincent Gaddis used it in a 1964 feature in Argosy magazine. In this article he had stated that Flight 19 and other similar disappearances were part of a strange pattern in this particular area. Many other articles followed soon after. Do you know that the Bermuda Triangle is one of the busiest areas which ships and aircrafts use!

Perhaps the most famous disappearance that had taken place in the Bermuda Triangle is that of Flight 19. On December 5, 1945, five US Navy Avenger bombers vanished mysteriously while they were on a routine training mission over the area. Lieutenant Charles Taylor led this flight training and he was constantly in contact on the radio with the base and then suddenly nothing could be heard. A rescue plane was sent fearing that the aircrafts and its crew were in trouble. But the rescue plane too vanished without a trace. That day, six aircrafts and 27 men had disappeared and they were never found. This disappearance in particular gave Bermuda Triangle its present reputation.

Some people however believe that the area of the Bermuda Triangle extends much farther than it is actually thought. It is so because of another mysterious disappearance of a cargo ship The Marie Celeste. The Marie Celeste left New York Harbour on November 5, 1872 loaded with a cargo of industrial alcohol. There were but a few passengers on board including Captain Benjamin Spooner Briggs, his wife and two year-old daughter and eight crew members. The same day that the Marie Celeste had left the harbour, it was found adrift in the Atlantic Ocean. All of its passengers and a life boat were missing. However the cargo and the personal belongings of all its passengers were on the ship. It was clear that the ship was abandoned quickly but why? This is one question that has not been answered.

Such like mysteries have continued to trouble many regarding the Bermuda Triangle. Various theories have been put forth to explain these disappearances ranging from methane emissions, UFO's, bad weather, rogue waves and even whirlpools. However, human error has not been ruled out in all these incidents.

A large number of the disappearances are said to have taken place due to the presence of large field of methane hydrates. Experiments have shown that these bubbles can cause a ship to sink rapidly. Another popular theory is the abduction by the aliens. Though there are many who would argue this has happened, is highly unlikely. However, violent storms called hurricanes or cyclones can destroy a ship or an airplanes in minutes, these violent storms grow in the seawater.

Whirlpools are found in many parts of the world. So another theory concerning the whirlpools comes into being. This force of nature can attract anything that comes in its range and cause it to sink. Gulf Stream, which passes through this area, too is thought to be the cause of the disappearance of the vessels. Besides all that is said and done, human error while controlling an aircraft or sailing a ship has not been ruled out. Misjudgements by humans while managing a vessel can also cause it to sink or crash. Did you know that compasses behave differently when they enter the Bermuda Triangle!

Though we have a number of theories to explain the disappearances of the Bermuda Triangle, but none of them give us a complete answer our questions. It has also been found that the disappearances in the Bermuda Triangle have also been exaggerated. Though a scare has been raised about the Bermuda Triangle but the area is used each day to travel by ships and by both commercial and private planes.

Complete the sentences

Read the sentences given below and complete them with the help of the chapter.

1. The Bermuda Triangle is mysterious ....
2. The most famous disappearance is Bermuda Triangle ....
   ....
3. Marie Celeste, a cargo ship was ....
   ....
4. Various versions including ....
   .... have been given to explain the disappearances in the Bermuda Triangle.
5. Methane Emissions can cause ....
   ....
6. Human error while .... can cause the disappearances.

Pick the correct answer

Choose the correct answers from the multiple choices given.

1. The Bermuda Triangle lies in the......................
   a. The Pacific Ocean   b. North Atlantic Ocean
   c. The Arctic Ocean
2. Bermuda Triangle is also called.............
   a. Devil's Playground   b. Devil's Triangle
   c. Devil's Workshop

98

3. The most famous flight disappearance in Bermuda Triangle is of ....
   a. Flight 21　　　　　　　　　b. Flight 91
   c. Flight 19

4. .... act differently in the Bermuda Triangle.
   a. Radars　　　　　　　　　　b. Compasses
   c. Motors

Punctuation

Read the following sentences given below. Use the capital letters, commas and full stops in these sentences wherever required. Then write the sentences in the space provided.

1. the cat has got stuck on the tree

   ....

2. mr smith went to africa to see an elephant

   ....

3. martha and her sister natasha take singing lessons

   ....

4. toby collected shells conch and a starfish at the beach

   ....

5. mother baked a cake prepared lemonade made sandwiches and fried fies for tina's friends

   ....

6. father was a soccer player in his school

   ....

7. neil went to visit his cousin pablo in barcelona

   ....

8. mario and philis on weekends took taekwondo classes
....

Read the word 'Triangle' given below on the first step of the ladder. Now, you must write five more words on the remaining steps. Remember that each new word must begin with the last letter of the previous word.

| TRIANGLE |

Your dog is lost! Everyone in your house is worried. Look for clues around the house of your dog. We hope you have found your dog. Now write on your notebook how you found your dog.

Fun to Know

18 **A warming up discussion**
- On which last occasion did you click photographs?
- When, according to you, was camera invented?

Camera

Camera, a device that allows us to capture precious moment spent with our friends and loved ones, is a remarkable invention. You too must now and then take photographs using a camera. But do you know when the camera was first made and what was the first ever photograph taken using a camera?

A camera is a lightproof enclosed device with an aperture and a shuttered lens used to take photographs. Cameras were invented centuries ago. Ibn-Al-Haythem (Alhazen) an Arabic Scientist had invented the first camera called the Pinhole Camera or Camera Obscura. He was also able to explain why the images appeared upside down. But back then the camera was not used for taking pictures but was rather used to draw pictures. Do you know that Camera Obscura means a 'Dark Room'?

But years and years passed by and it was only in 1814 that a Frenchman Joseph Nicephore Niepce managed to take the first photograph using the Camera Obscura. But it took eight hours of exposure in the sun for the photograph to develop and it soon faded! The heliographs or sun prints, the name given to his photographs, became the model for modern photographs. It is so because he had used light to draw the photographs.

A few years later in 1837, a French artist Jacques Mandé Daguerre invented the Daguerreotype. It was an effective method of photography. Daguerre's process 'fixed' the images onto a sheet of silver-plated copper. He polished the silver and coated it with iodine and thus created a surface that was sensitive to light. He put this plate in a camera and left it exposed for a few minutes. After the image was painted by light, Daguerre bathed the plate in a solution of silver chloride. And a lasting image was created. Thus, the era of photography had started. Interestingly, by 1850 New York alone had over 70 studios that used daguerreotype cameras!

Do you know that in 1843, a photograph was used in an advertisement for the first time! Photography had also become popular with the invention of negatives. They were made by English botanist and mathematician Henry Fox Talbot. He had his technique of Calotype patented which involved the negative-positive print making. Through this process, multiple copies of the image could be made. In this process, he sensitized paper to light with a silver salt solution. He then exposed the paper to light. The background became black, and the subject was shown in shades of grey. This was a negative image and from the paper negative Talbot made contact prints, reversing the light and shadows to create a detailed picture. As time passed by, more and more invention and improvements were made in the field of camera, and capturing photographs became extremely popular.

And then, in 1880, George Eastman came on the scene with his box cameras. His cameras were called Kodak Cameras. He sold the cameras manufactured by his company with a film inside that allowed the buyer to take 100 photographs. When the photographs had been taken, the camera was sent to the company, where the photographs were processed and the photographs along with a new film in the camera were returned to the buyer. A year later, the delicate paper film used for photographs was changed to a plastic base. In 1889, George Eastman invented a film roll that was flexible, unbreakable and could be rolled. And thus box cameras started getting manufactured on a large scale.

Flashbulbs were later invented to provide more light while the photographs are taken. Then in 1913-14 came the 35mm Cameras that allowed the photographs to be enlarged after they had been exposed. Later, as cameras became more popular, the Eastman Kodak company started selling Kodak chrome film in the market.

By the 1940s, colour films were launched. These films used the technology of dye-coupled colours in which a chemical process connected the three dye layers of red blue and green together and thus created a colour image. Another invention in the 1940s of instant photograph by using Polaroid cameras brought photography to a new level. Polaroid cameras became a rage as photographs could be developed instantly. Interestingly, the first photograph of our planet was taken in 1968 from the moon!

Further inventions in the field of camera happened. And in 1984, Canon came out with the first digital electronic still camera. And so, the cameras had revolutionized the world by allowing to capture what we saw around us instantly and to treasure it.

Do you know that today there are 2.5 billion people around the world that use cameras!

 **Let's remember the story**

Answer the following questions.

1. Who invented the first cameras and what were they called?
2. What was the achievement of Joseph Nicephore Niepce?
3. Why did negative films become popular?
4. Box cameras had become very famous. Why?
5. What was the technique used behind coloured film roles?
6. Why had Polaroid cameras become a rage?

Prefixes and suffixes

Given below are a few prefixes and suffixes along with a number of words. Use them together to make new words.

anti-	be-	en-	-er	-able	-ness

| Pathy | come | close | dote | body | little | tangle | tomb | social |
| fore | calm | slave | thesis | side | deck | twine | amor | septic |

....

....

....

....

Word steps

Read the word 'Camera' given below on the first step of the ladder. Now, you must write five more words on the remaining steps. Remember that each new word must begin with the last letter of the previous word.

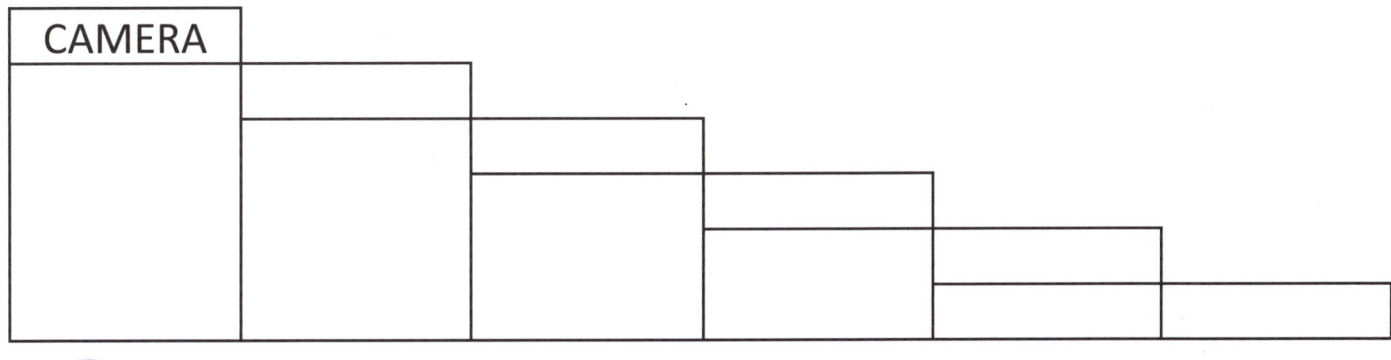

Idioms

Match the idioms given in Column A with their meanings in Column B.

Idioms	Meanings
Use one's loaf	To loose the energy to continue
The ball is in your court	To die
Run out of steam	Undecided about something
On the fence	To use one's common sense
Kick the bucket	To study
Hit the books	You need to take action

 **Scavenger hunt**

Give the children a letter and ask them to photograph as many things as possible beginning with that particular letter within a definite time frame. Whosoever gets the maximum number of photographs is the winner.

Fun to Know

19 **A warming up discussion**
- What kind of animals have you seen at the zoo?
- Which is the largest animal you have seen at the zoo?

At the Zoo

There are lions and roaring tigers,
and enormous camels and things,
There are biffalo-buffalo-bisons,
and a great big bear with wings.
There's a sort of a tiny potamus,
and a tiny nosserus too -
But I gave buns to the elephant
when I went down to the Zoo!

There are badgers and bidgers and bodgers,
and a Super-in-tendent's House,
There are masses of goats, and a Polar,
and different kinds of mouse,
And I think there's a sort of a something
which is called a wallaboo -
But I gave buns to the elephant
when I went down to the Zoo!
If you try to talk to the bison,
he never quite understands;
You can't shake hands with a mingo -
he doesn't like shaking hands.
And lions and roaring tigers
hate saying, 'How do you do?' -
But I give buns to the elephant
when I go down to the Zoo!

Complete the sentences

Read the sentences given below and complete them with the help of the poem.

1. The narrator gave..
   ....

2. A bison never ....
   ....

3. A few animals mentioned in the poem are ....
   ....

4. Lions and tigers do not..
   ....

5. Narrators experiences of visiting the zoo are ....
   ....
   ....
   ....
   ....

6. Two different kinds of bears mentioned in the poem are ....
   ....

Practise writing sentences

Use the following words in your own sentences.

1. Enormous

   ....

2. Super

   ....

3. Kind

   ....

4. Different

   ....

5. Hate

   ....

6. Buns

   ....

Think and fill

Read the following sentences. Fill in the blanks using the correct articles, *a*, *an*, and *the*.

1. ....alligator is............ reptile.
2. Do not move............. books from the table.
3. He goes to............. gym each day.
4. John wishes for............. new car.
5. He brought............. letter.
6. .... milk inside the jug was hot.
7. He has............. dog and............ parrot for his pet.
8. She is performing in.............. play at school.

Crossword

With the help of given clues, complete the crossword.

Across

1. It is the largest land animal
4. A place where animals are kept
5. A large animal that often steals honey

Down

1. Something which is very, very big
2. It roars and has a mane
3. It is the ship of the desert

 **At the zoo**

You must have visited a zoo. What have been your experiences at the zoo? Write in the lines provided below.

....
....
....
....
....
....
....
....
....
....

Fun to Know

20 **A warming up discussion**
- Have you been troubled with rats?
- What have you done to get rid of them?

The Pied Piper of Hamelin

Once upon a time there was a town named Hamelin in Germany. It was a port town on the River Weser. It would have been like any other town had it not been tormented by the numerous rats in the city. There were rats everywhere in Hamelin. They were found in the streets, in the houses, under the bed, on the table and in the cabinets as well. These rats ate the cheese, bit the people and even chased the dogs and cats. The people couldn't bake a cake, take a bath or sleep in their beds without the rats joining in. The rats even nibbled on the ears of babies sleeping in their cots.

The people could find no means to get rid of the rats! They were hopeless and obsessed with the thought of rats troubling them.

One day, the people of Hamelin made their way to the Town Square and knocked on the big brass doors of the Town Hall and demanded to know what the Mayor was doing about the rats. The Mayor appeared on the balcony in his black robes.

'Good citizens of Hamelin, you may rest assured that what needs to be done is being done. Don't you worry about that,' said the Mayor. But the people kept repeating that nothing was done to make Hamelin free of rats. The Mayor became nervous. He then asked his councillors what must be done to get rid of the rats.

Then, the Mayor announced that he would give one thousand gold coins to anyone who would get Hamelin free of rats. The next day, a stranger appeared in Hamelin. He wore clothes that were half yellow and half red. He was long and thin with long hair and sparkling blue eyes. And from a scarf around him, there hung a silver pipe. He went straight to the Mayor who was sitting with his councillors.

'I can make Hamelin free of rats for one thousand gold coins,' the Pied Piper said to the Mayor.

'Of course, you shall be given that amount,' said the Mayor enthusiastically.

At once, the Pied Piper went out. He reached the square and looked quietly around. He took a deep breath and blew a note on his silver pipe that spoke to the rats of far off places, of woods and forests and rocks and mountains. He blew another note and a soft mumbling was heard everywhere. Then, he blew a third note and began to play his pipe in earnest.

In no time, the mumbling turned to grumbling and then it became a great rumbling. And as the people of Hamelin looked on, rats from everywhere came hurrying and scurrying to the square where the Pied Piper stood playing his pipe. There were all kinds of rats, small rats, big rats, fat rats, brown rats and in general rats of every kind were tumbling over each

other to reach the Pied Piper.

When the rats had gathered around him, the Pied Piper began walking out of the town still playing his pipe. And surprisingly, the rats followed the Pied Piper hurrying and tumbling over each other. The people astonished looked on. The Pied Piper led the rats out of Hamelin and towards River Weser. At the riverbank, the Piper dipped one of his toes into the water. At once, the rats started jumping into the river and were drowned. When all the rats had drowned, the Piped Piper stopped playing his pipe. There were no rats in Hamelin now! People were rejoicing.

The Pied Piper then went to the Mayor and asked for his one thousand gold coins. 'One thousand gold coins!' cried the Mayor. 'That is too much. We all saw that as the rats drowned themselves all you did was stand by the river and play your pipe. I will give you fifty gold coins and be satisfied with that sum of money.'

To the Pied Piper's disappointment, everyone in the town seemed to agree with the Mayor. Some even started laughing at the Pied Piper.

'You must pay me the one thousand gold coins or I shall play another tune on my pipe and then you all shall be sorry,' said the Pied Piper angrily.

'Do what you want,' said the mayor. 'We shall pay you nothing.'

And so once again, the Pied Piper was seen standing in the square. Once more, he put his silver pipe to his lips and began playing it. And this time, the melody was quite different. First there was a hustling, then there was a bustling and then the people saw their children coming towards the Pied Piper. The children were laughing and singing. The people were horrified. They tried to stop their children but couldn't.

Even the Mayor's daughter was among the children.

When all the children had gathered, the Pied Piper once again started walking out of the town. But this time, he went towards the mountains. The children merrily followed him. When they were out of the town, suddenly a door opened in one of the mountains and the Pied Piper led the children through that door and into the mountain. When all the children were inside, the door closed itself. The people stood stunned unable to do anything.

The people were grief-stricken. Suddenly, they saw a lame child coming towards them. They asked him where the others had gone. All that he said was, 'The Pied Piper had promised to take us to a wonderful land where fruit trees grew and the rivers gushed. Alas! I cannot see that land!'

The people never saw their children again neither did they saw the Pied Piper. And after that day, the people of Hamelin always paid their dues on time.

Let's remember the story

Answer the following questions.

1. Why were the people of Hamelin troubled?
2. Why and what reward was announced by the Mayor of Hamelin?
3. How did the Pied Piper got rid of the rats?
4. Why did the Mayor refused to pay the Pied Piper?
5. How did the Pied Piper punish the people of Hamelin?
6. What did the lame boy tell the people of Hamelin?

Circling the words

Read the passage given below carefully and put a circle around the verbs.

He went to the seashore and shouted his speech out to the sea. He also kept pebbles in his mouth. By doing so, he had to struggle to bring out every sound. After a while when he spoke without the stones, the words came out of his mouth loud and clear. Later, he watched himself speak before the mirror which led him to improve his actions, gestures and expressions. He continued to practice his speech on the seashore. Each time he spoke louder so that his words could be heard over the roaring waves. While climbing the hill too, he continued to speak out his speech and thus controlled his breath, his voice and his tone.

Phrases, here we come!

Read the sentences below carefully and complete them with help of the phrases given in the box.

| Come what may | as old as the hills | on cloud nine |
| at loggerheads | mad as a hatter | neither here nor there |

1. That house down the street is...

2. Ethan decided to learn Portuguese..

3. When Sara got her scholarship, she was...

4. The Smiths and Jacksons are... with each other.

5. Even after driving for six hours, Sam was still..

6. When Toby broke the porcelain vase, mom was...

Dialogue writing

Write a short dialogue between you and your friend. You are inviting your best friend over the weekend for a camping trip with your parents. Or write a short dialogue where you tell your friend how much you have enjoyed the weekend camping with your parents.

Word steps

Read the word 'CAMERA' given below on the first step of the ladder. Now, write five more words on the remaining steps. Remember that each new word should begin with the last letter of the previous word.

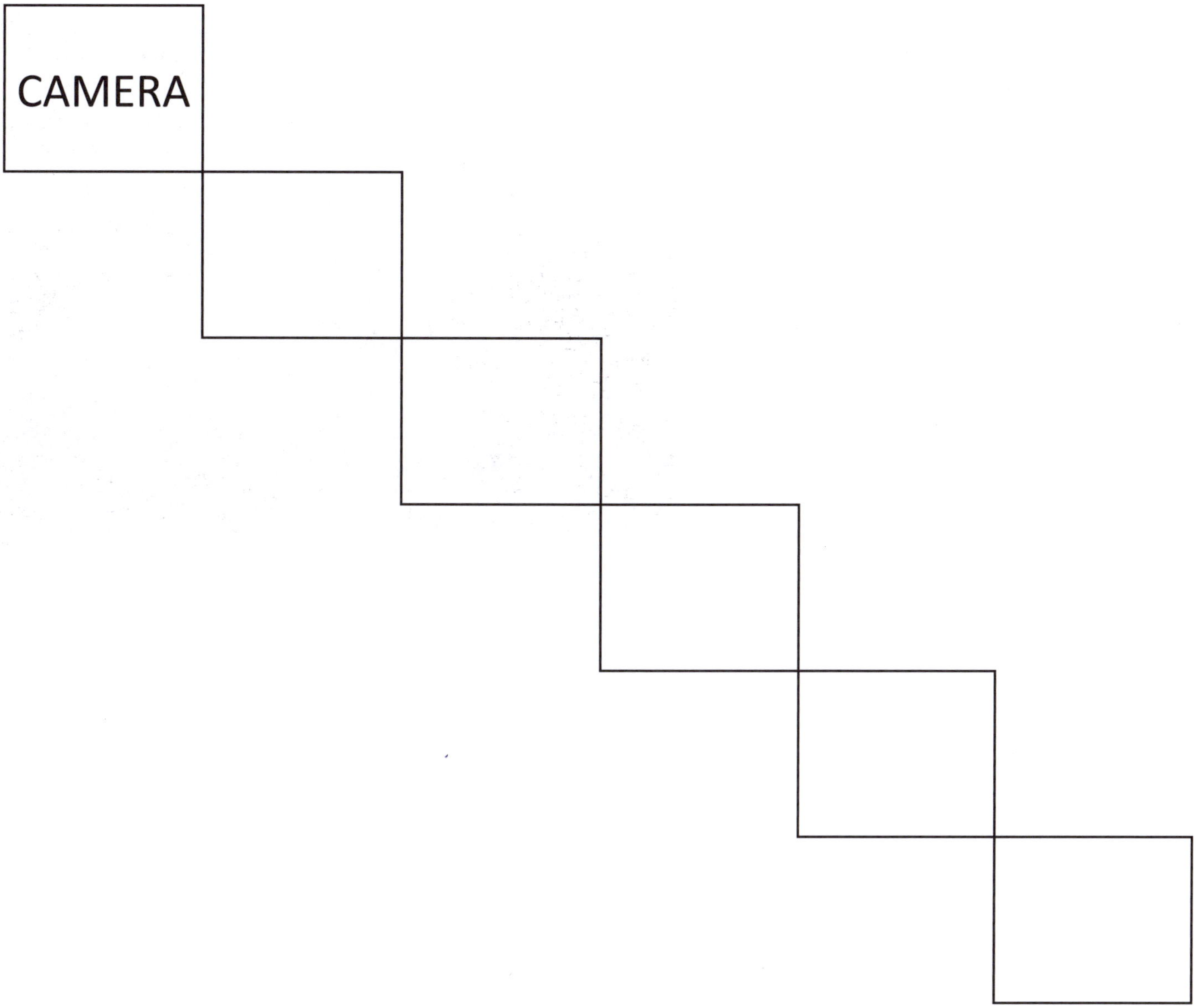

CAMERA

Fun to Know

A warming up discussion
- What kind of an animal is an octopus?
- What do you know about an octopus?

Octopus

You must have seen an octopus. But do you know about the various unique abilities that this creature has! Octopus is considered among the most mysterious creatures on the earth. It is because of its abilities and also due to the way it lives.

Octopuses are found around the world especially in the coral reefs and on the ocean floor. An octopus has no bones in its body and so it belongs to the family of invertebrates. Octopuses that are found in warm waters are often small. Large octopuses are found in cold waters. Do you know that octopuses only live for 1-2 years!

An octopus has a large bulbous head, a set of big eyes and eight arms with two rows of suckers on each arm. The arms of the octopus also allow the creature to grab and eat its prey. It has a parrot like beak to eat its food. It has excellent eyesight even in the dark but it cannot hear. Were you aware that an octopus has three hearts! Its blood is also light blue in colour. Do you know that octopus swim backwards by blasting water through a muscular tube in their body called siphon!

There are over 300 species of octopus in the world. They all vary in size and colour but they have their unique abilities in common. Octopus has an array of mechanism using which it can save itself from its predators mostly sharks, eels and dolphins. Like a chameleon, an octopus can change its colour. But the octopus is much faster than a chameleon in doing so. Its body is covered with pigment cells and specialized muscles that hide the octopus by blending the colour of its skin with its surroundings. The predator is then unable to see the octopus.

If the octopus is discovered, he releases a jet of black ink and thus minimizing the view of its attacker. It then quickly runs away. The jet of black ink also contains a substance that dulls the sense of smell of the predator and makes it difficult to track the octopus. Do you know that fast swimming octopus can swim faster by expelling water at great speed through their mantles! Incredible! Isn't it?

If however, the predator is able to catch the octopus despite these mechanisms, an octopus can shed one of its arms to distract the predator and swim to safety. Also, as the creature had no bones in its body, it can even squeeze into small crevices and can enter small holes and dens to hide itself. It can also give a nasty bite to its predator using its parrot like beak and can also release venomous saliva to subdue its prey. Don't you think that octopus is an intelligent invertebrate!

Do you know that octopuses always hunt at night and that they disorient their prey before attacking it! Crabs, molluscs and cray fish are its favourite food. Despite their excellent defence mechanism, octopus is an intelligent problem solver. It has been known to climb fishing vessels and open the boxes containing crabs! Interestingly, octopuses collect crustacean shells to make gardens outside their dens.

Let's remember the story

Answer the following questions.

1. Why is the octopus considered a mysterious creature?
2. Describe the physical appearance of an octopus.

3. Where are these creatures found?

4. Name two methods by which an octopus can defend itself from its predators.

5. How does an octopus catch its prey?

6. Why are octopuses called 'problem solvers'?

Pick the correct answer

Choose the correct answers from the multiple choices given.

1. An octopus has two rows of........................ on its arms.
   a. Spines
   b. Suckers
   c. Fangs

2. An octopus swims ....
   a. Forwards
   b. Sideways
   c. Backwards

3. An octopus ejects a jet of............................ to fool its predator.
   a. Black ink
   b. Blue ink
   c. Red ink

4. An octopus collects crustacean shells to make........................... outside their den
   a. Garden
   b. Wall
   c. Radar

Let's hear your thoughts

In the chapter, you have learnt about the octopus. It belongs to the family of invertebrates. Find out the special features of the invertebrates and write them in the space provided.

....

....

....

....

....

....

Think and fill

Read the following sentences. Fill in the blanks using the correct articles, *a*, *an*, and *the*.

1. He has decided to go to........ city of San Francisco.

2. He left our house at........... quarter to one.

3. I would like to eat............ ice cream and......... piece of cake.

4. Let's have......... cup of tea.

5. She returned to............ reading room and waited for her friend.

6. Every morning, he goes for........... walk.

7. They stood admiring.............. hills before them.

8. He went to............ store looking for a particular vase.

Fun to Know

A warming up discussion
- Do you play pranks on others?
- Have you ever got in trouble for playing your prank?

Tom Sawyer

Saturday morning was bright, fresh and brimming with life. Cardiff Hill, beyond the village and above it, was green and seemed dreamy, reposeful, and inviting. Tom appeared on the sidewalk with a bucket of whitewash and a long-handled brush. As he surveyed the fence, all gladness left him. Before him was thirty yards of board fence, nine feet high and Tom was depressed.

With a deep sigh, he dipped his brush and passed it along one of the planks; repeated the operation. Then, he stepped back and compared the insignificant whitewashed streak with the far-reaching continent of unwhitewashed fence. Seeing the vastness of his work, Tom sat down on a tree-box discouraged.

Jim came skipping out at the gate with a tin pail. He was bringing water from the town pump, a hateful work in Tom's eyes, but now it seemed interesting.

Tom said, 'Jim, I'll fetch the water if you'll whitewash.'

Jim shook his head and said that he had been forbidden by Aunt Polly to help him and that she would be supervising him herself. Tom tried to bribe Jim but the timely arrival of Aunt Polly prevented Tom from passing on his earned privilege.

Once gain, Tom set to whitewash but his energy did not last. He began to think of the fun he had planned for this day and his sorrows multiplied. He got out his worldly wealth and examined it—bits of toys, marbles, and trash; enough to buy an exchange of work, maybe, but not half enough to buy so much as half an hour of pure freedom. So with a sigh, he returned his things to his pocket and gave up the idea of trying to buy the boys. It was at this dark and hopeless moment that an inspiration burst upon crafty Tom!

Immediately, he took up his brush and went tranquilly to work. Ben Rogers appeared—the very boy, whose ridicule he had been dreading. Ben took light steps as he munched his apple and sang a deep-toned ding-dong-dong, ding-dong- dong, for he was personating a steamboat. Suddenly, he stopped singing and stared ahead with his mouth open. Tom Sawyer was working! He drew nearer to Tom.

Tom went on whitewashing—paying no attention to Ben's playfulness as a steamboat. Ben stared a moment and then said, 'Hi-YI! You're up a stump, aren't you?'

No answer. Tom surveyed his last touch with the eye of an artist, and then giving his brush another gentle sweep he surveyed the result, as before. Ben ran up alongside of him. Ben said, 'Hello, old chap, you got to work, hey?'

Tom wheeled suddenly and said, 'Why, it's you, Ben! I wasn't noticing.'

'I'm going swimming. Don't you wish you could? But of course you'd rather work—wouldn't you? Course you would!'

Tom contemplated the boy a bit, and said, 'What do you call work?'

'Why, isn't that work?'

Tom resumed his whitewashing, and answered carelessly, 'Well, maybe it is, and maybe it isn't. All I know is it suits Tom Sawyer.'

'Oh come, now, you don't mean to say that you like it?'

'Like it? Well, I don't see why I oughtn't to like it. Does a boy get a chance to whitewash a fence every day?'

That put the thing in a new light for Ben. He stopped nibbling his apple. Tom swept his brush daintily back and forth—stepped back to note the effect—added a touch here and there-and Ben watched every move and got more and more interested, more and more absorbed. At last, he said, 'Say, Tom, let me whitewash a little.'

'No—no—Ben. You see, Aunt Polly's awfully particular about this fence—right here on the street, it's got to be done very carefully,' said Tom.

'Now let me just try. Only a little—I'd let you, if you was me, Tom.'

'Ben, I'd like to, honestly; but Aunt Polly—well, Jim and Sid wanted to do it, but she wouldn't let them do it. If you tried and anything happened to it—'

'Oh, I'll be just as careful. Now let me try. Say—I'll give you the core of my apple.'

'Well, here—No, Ben, now don't. I'm afraid—'

'I'll give you all of it!'

Tom gave up the brush with reluctance in his face but alacrity in his heart. And while the late steamer Big Missouri worked and sweated in the sun, the retired artist sat on a barrel in the shade close by, munched his apple, and planned the slaughter of more innocents.

There was no lack of material; for boys came to jeer but remained to whitewash. By the time Ben was tired, Tom had traded the next chance to Billy Fisher for a kite; and when he was exhausted, Johnny Miller bought in a chance for a dead rat and a string to swing it with—and so on, and so on, and hour after hour. And when the middle of the afternoon came, from being a poor poverty-stricken boy in the morning, Tom was literally rolling in wealth.

He had a nice, good, idle time all the while as the fence got three coats of the whitewash done. If he hadn't run out of whitewash, Tom would have bankrupted every boy in the village. Tom said to himself that it was not such a hollow world, after all. He had discovered that in order to make a man or boys covet a thing, it is only necessary to make the thing difficult to attain. Crafty Tom then went towards headquarters to report his accomplishment.

Let's remember the story

Answer the following questions.

1. Why was Tom disappointed?
2. Why did Jim refuse to help Tom?
3. Who came to tease Tom? What was he impersonating?
4. How did Tom convince Ben to paint the fence?
5. Which treasured possessions did Tom take from the boys?
6. 'Tom would have bankrupted every boy in the village'. Explain this statement.

Prepositions

Fill in the blanks using the prepositions given below.

| except   under   in   among   to   inside   upon   behind |

1. The ball had rolled .... the table.

2. The flowers were kept .... the vase.

3. The children are playing .... the trees.

4. Larry is hiding .... his mother.

5. Noel and Joe like .... spend time playing the video games.

6. They kept the fish .... the grocer's bag.

7. Everyone came to the party .... Sam.

8. Mother kept the suitcase .... the bed.

Let's hear your thoughts

Write a few sentences about Tom. What kind of a boy, do you think, is he?

....

....

....

....

....

....

....

....

Share your plate of mischief

Write the funniest thing that you have ever done.

....

....

....

....

....

....

....

....

Fun to Know

23 A warming up discussion
- Have you ever been to a forest?
- Which most extraordinary thing did you see there?

Stopping by Woods on a Snowy Evening

Whose woods these are I think I know.

His house is in the village, though;

He will not see me stopping here

To watch his woods fill up with snow.

My little horse must think it queer

To stop without a farmhouse near

Between the woods and frozen lake

The darkest evening of the year.

He gives his harness bells a shake

To ask if there is some mistake.

The only other sound's the sweep

Of easy wind and downy flake.

The woods are lovely, dark and deep,

But I have promises to keep,

And miles to go before I sleep,

And miles to go before I sleep.

(Robert Frost)

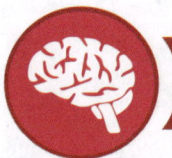

Let's remember the story

Answer the following questions.

1. What is the setting of the poem?
2. At what place does the narrator stops?
3. What is the poet talking about in the third stanza?
4. List the adjectives that have been used to describe the woods.
5. Explain 'And miles to go before I sleep'.
6. Which sounds can be heard in the poem?

Synonyms

Match the words with their synonyms given in the following table.

Words	Synonyms
Woods	Icy
Queer	Unlit
Frozen	Strange
Mistake	Forest
Dark	Error

Practise writing sentences

Use the following words in your own sentences.

1. Queer

   ....

2. Harness

   ....

3. Wind

   ....

4. Promise

   ....

5. Deep

   ....

6. Frozen

   ....

g) Circling the words

Read the passage given below carefully and put a circle around the adjectives.

She put on the *pretty* *silk* dress and went outside. She also had the *new* sunshade on her head. People turned to look at her. She wondered whether people thought her *strange*. But they were actually admiring her *lovely* sunshade. They continued to talk about the *beautiful* stranger even after she had passed by.

She went to the *big* park where the *popular* band played every Friday. Once there, she saw the park decorated with *bright* lights and people dancing to *melodious* music. She was always *shy* to dance but today somehow she was filled with confidence. She stepped forward and began dancing, spinning her *blue* sunshade in her hands.

Fun to Know

24

A warming up discussion
- What is a National Park?
- Have you ever visited a National Park?

Yellowstone National Park

Would you not like to visit a place where you could not only enjoy yourself but also learn and examine things? Can you think of a park where you can go snow boarding, boating, camping and hiking one after the other? Think again of a place where you can see numerous geysers, hot springs and mud pots and also mountains and a volcano! Such an area with some of these features would be called a national park. However, Yellowstone National Park, the oldest national park has all of the above.

Yellowstone is a National Park. A National Park is a large area of land that is preserved and protected for its scenic beauty, environmental and historical importance. Yellowstone National Park is known for its wildlife, geological features and its scenic beauty. It is located primarily in Wyoming (96%) but some portions of the park also fall into Idaho (1%) and Montana (3%). Do you know that Yellowstone National Park is larger in area than Rhode Island and Delaware combined!

It was established in 1872 after American geologist Ferdinand V. Hayden had convinced the Congress that Yellowstone area needs to be protected and preserved for its wildlife, its environmental and geological features. Yellowstone thus became the first National Park in the world. Today, among the world's most visited National Parks, Yellowstone has so much for those who come to visit. Interestingly, most of the park is volcanic in nature while the remaining part is sedimentary.

Yellowstone is famous worldwide for its geysers, mud pots and hot springs. Do you know that there are more than 300 geysers in Yellowstone National Park! This makes about 1/3 of all the geysers that are found in the world. The Old Faithful geyser is the most famous of the geysers of the park. It shoots out 8,500 gallons of water in each of its eruption. The Riverside Geyser is another known geyser and it erupts after every six hours. Apart from its geysers, the park is also known for its hot springs. A key attraction of the park, Grand Prismatic Spring is the third largest hot spring in the world! This hot spring is brightly coloured because of the bacteria and microbial mats that grow around the mineral rich water.

Besides hot springs and geysers, Yellowstone National Park also has over

240 waterfalls and a number of mud spots. Forests also form an important part of the park. Six forests make the ecosystem of this National Park. On an estimate 80% of the park is covered with forests. These forests are home to 67 species of animals ranging from elk, grizzly bear, bison, wolves, mountain lions, moose, beavers, trumpeter swans, eagles, white pelicans and coyotes. These animals play an important role in the ecosystem of Yellowstone National Park. The subalpine forests in the park are also home to about 1350 species of plants and trees. With such a rich variety of wildlife, Yellowstone provides its visitors an opportunity to photograph various animals in their natural environment. Do you know that Yellowstone National Park is the only place after California in the US that experiences most number of earthquakes!

Though it is covered with forests, mountains and lakes that increase the scenic beauty of the park, Yellowstone National Park is basically volcanic in nature. It is because the world's largest caldera is in this park. The caldera is about 45 miles by 30 miles in area. The caldera is considered to be an active volcano. The volcano has erupted with great force a few times in the last two million years.

Do you know that humans have been living in the park for about the last 11,000 years! Well, the Native Americans have certainly been living here in harmony with the environment of the park. But today, it has become necessary to preserve and protect Yellowstone National Park from the vast number of visitors that come here. Forest fires, either from human or natural causes, also threaten this diverse ecosystem. The forest fire of 1988 destroyed 1/3 of it. However, efforts have been made to check the spread of wildfires and to protect the wildlife of the area.

Yellowstone National Park, the world's oldest park has unique features. It is an ideal place to study geothermal activity, a place to witness the awesome power of geysers, to see and explore a rich variety of wildlife and a wide array of flora. Yellowstone National Park also offers a large range of recreational facilities from hiking, camping, boating, sightseeing, snowboarding and snow mobiles. It is because of this that Yellowstone

National Park remains one of the most visited and the most famous national parks in the world.

Let's remember the story

Answer the following questions.

1. What is a national park?
2. Where is the Yellow Stone National Park located?
3. Why is the Yellow Stone National Park famous?
4. Why is the Yellow Stone National Park called a photographer's paradise?
5. Yellow Stone National Park is volcanic in nature. Explain.
6. Which are the threats to the Yellow Stone National Park?

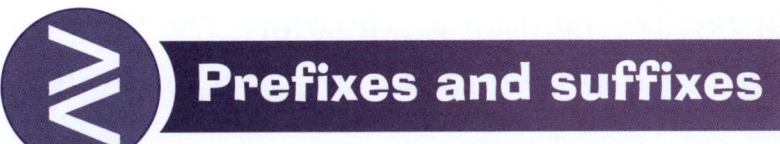

Prefixes and suffixes

Given below are a few prefixes and suffixes along with a number of words. Use them together to make new words.

-dom	-er	-less	un-			
Free	wide	martyr	friend	official	tire	foreign
grand	self	play	low	king	soon	meaning

....

....

....

....

136

Widen your horizon

Yellowstone National Park is famous for its geysers. Find out about some of its famous geysers and write what you have found out in the space given below.

....

....

....

....

....

....

....

Fun to Know

A warming up discussion
- Have you seen a puppet show?
- What kind of a puppet would you want for yourself?

The Four Puppets

There once lived a gifted puppet maker. He had a son called Aung. The puppet maker thought that his son would follow his profession but that was not to be.

'Father,' said Aung one day, 'I've decided to seek my fortune elsewhere.'

The puppet maker was saddened hearing this. 'I wish you would stay, my son,' said the puppeteer. 'But if you must leave, take these companions with you.'

He then showed his son four wooden puppets he had carved, painted, and costumed. 'Each puppet,' he said, 'has its own virtue. The first puppet was the king of the gods. His virtue is wisdom. The second puppet is a green ogre. His virtue is strength. The third is a sorcerer and knowledge is his virtue. The hermit comes last with his goodness. These virtues can help you on your way.

But remember, strength and knowledge must always serve wisdom and goodness.' With his father's blessings, Aung started his journey with the four puppets tied to his bamboo pole.

As night fell, Aung stopped beneath a banyan tree in a forest. He said, 'I wonder if this place is safe. Let me ask the king.'

To his surprise, the moment he asked the puppet, it became alive, came down from the pole and said, 'Aung, open your eyes and look around. Its the first step to wisdom. If you fail to see what is right before you, people will easily misguide you.'

The next moment, the puppet was again hanging from the pole. Composing himself, Aung looked around and saw tiger foot prints on the ground. He decided to sleep on a tree branch. He was glad for doing so for at midnight a tiger did came prowling below him. The next day, by evening, Aung camped high up the mountainside. Next morning, when he woke up, he saw a caravan coming along the road below. A dozen bullock carts were piled high with costly goods.

'That caravan must belong to some rich merchant,' Aung thought. 'I wish I had wealth like that.'

Then, he asked the green-faced ogre, 'Tell me, how can I gain such riches?'

The puppet of the ogre too came to life and said, 'If you have strength,' bellowed he, 'you can take whatever you like.!' And before Aung could stop him, he stamped his foot forcefully causing a landslide. The caravan was trapped between boulders. Frightened, the cart drivers ran off. Aung then took the carts for his own.

'All of this is mine!' he said filled with wonder.

Then, Aung heard a sob. Lying huddled in one of the carts was a lovely young woman. She was crying and was terrified.

'I won't hurt you,' said Aung gently. 'Who are you?'

'My name is Mala,' she said in a small voice. 'My father is the owner of this caravan. We were on our way to meet him.'

139

Meanwhile, Aung had fallen in love with Mala. He wanted to marry Mala. 'Don't worry,' he said. 'I'll take you with me and care for you.'

Hearing this, Mala grew angry. She refused to marry him and decided to never talk to Aung. Aung was shocked. Just then, the ogre persuaded Aung not to worry for sooner or later, she will forget her anger. The ogre then cleared the road and then helped Aung lead the caravan. Soon, they were near the capital city.

Aung asked the ogre, 'What should I do with all these riches?'

'Ask the sorcerer!' said the ogre. And so Aung asked the sorcerer.

The puppet came to life, as Mala looked on with wide eyes, and said, 'If you want your wealth to grow you must learn the secrets of nature.'

Then, the sorcerer tapped his wand and he and Aung flew into the air. Aung saw which land was fertile and where treasures were hidden. He decided to help the people but the sorcerer persuaded him to keep the knowledge to himself.

And so, Aung came to the capital city. He became a merchant and counselled from time to time with the ogre and the sorcerer. Soon, he was many times richer. He bought a palace for himself and Mala, and kept the puppets in a special room. But he wasn't happy for Mala never talked to him and remained aloof. One day, he discovered that Mala had run away.

Aung was shocked. In despair, he cried, 'What good is all my wealth if I've lost what I care for the most?'

For once, the ogre and the sorcerer were silent and still. Aung then remembered the hermit's puppet who he had never called. Turning to the hermit, he asked, 'Why has everything gone wrong?'

The puppet came to life like the others. The hermit said, 'Aung, you imagined that wealth brings happiness. But true happiness comes only from goodness. What is important is not what you have but what you do with it.'

The king of the gods then came to life and stood beside the hermit. 'You forgot what your father had told you, Aung. Strength and knowledge are useful but they must always serve wisdom and goodness.'

From that day on, Aung used his wealth to do good. He built a splendid holy pagoda, and offered food and shelter to those who visited the shrine. One day among the visitors, Aung saw a young woman he knew well. An older man stood beside her. It was Mala and her father. The next moment, he knelt before the old man and said, 'Sir, I have done you great wrong. I beg your forgiveness. All I have is yours and I will give it up gladly. I will be content making puppets.'

'Father,' said Mala softly, 'this is Aung. But he has changed!'

'So it seems!' said her father. 'And if so, it would be unwise to let go of a young man of talent. Perhaps, he would like to work with me!'

So Aung became the merchant's assistant, and with time he won Mala's heart and they married. As for the puppets, Aung still called on them as needed. But though he was helped often by strength and knowledge, he was guided always by wisdom and goodness.

Let's remember the story

Answer the following questions.

1. What were the qualities of the puppets?
2. What was the king's advice to Aung?
3. How did the ogre help Aung get wealthy?
4. Why was Mala unhappy with Aung?
5. What was the hermit's advice to Aung?
6. Aung was a changed man at the end of the story. Explain.

Words and their meanings

Read the words given below. With the help of a dictionary find out their meanings and write in the table.

Words	Meanings
Virtue	
Misguide	
Caravan	
Counsel	
Splendid	
Secret	

Word ladder

Read the word 'Puppet' given below on the first step of the ladder. Now,

142

write five more words on the remaining steps. Remember that each new word should begin with the last letter of the previous word.

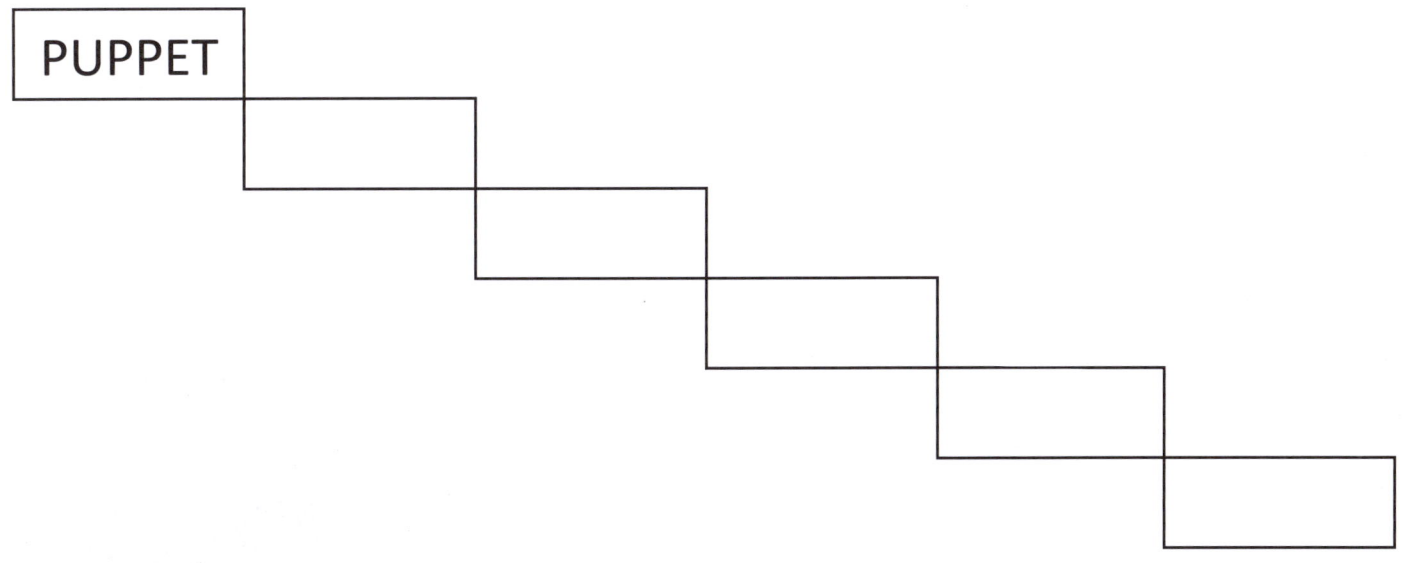

PUPPET

Puppet show

Puppets are a fun way to tell stories. Find out about puppets and write what you have found out in the space provided.

....

....

....

....

....

....

....

Fun to Know

A warming up discussion
- What do you know about Africa?
- Can you name one place that is in the African continent?

Africa

Africa—the word itself brings forth many varied reactions. Some think that Africa is where the tribes lives, some think of Africa in terms of only Egypt and its ancient civilization and cricket lovers might think of Africa as only consisting South Africa. But Africa encompasses all this and much more. From the vast Sahara Desert to the beautiful River Nile, the deep Congo Basin to the spectacular wildlife and breathtaking landscapes, Africa leaves one spell bound with its enriching culture, traditions, its geography and its history.

The African continent is the second largest continent in the world. This vast and diverse continent is surrounded by the Mediterranean Sea in the North, by the Suez Canal and the Red Sea in the northeast, by the Indian Ocean in the east and southeast and by the Atlantic Ocean in the west. It is because of its location that Africa offers its visitors a diverse variety of wildlife, climate and even terrain.

Do you know that Africa is the second most populous continent in the world! Most of the people in Africa still live in non-urban areas and only a few places or cities have adapted to modernization. Nigeria is by far the most populous country in Africa. Cairo in Egypt and Lagos in Nigeria are the two most populated cities in Africa. Interestingly, many of the African countries gained their freedom after World War II. Interestingly, more than 2000 languages are spoken in the African continent!

Have you ever heard that Africa is the oldest inhabited continent on earth! Africa is widely accepted as the place where the humans and the 'great apes' had originated. It is so because a great number of fossils of the earliest Hominids that date back to a few million years have been found only on the African continent. The early humans were hunters and they lived in caves. They had discovered fire and had developed stone tools which were the most important invention of the early man. The discovery of the partial skeleton of 'Lucy', an ancie in 1974 in Ethiopia sparked major research in the region regarding the life of early humans.

Besides being the cradle of civilization, Africa also boosts of a rich and enticing history. The Egyptian civilization stands out among the other civilizations of the world for its immense knowledge and achievements in the fields of architecture, agriculture, education and trade. The Great Pyramids and the Sphinx at Giza and several temples tell the tale of the glory of the Egyptian civilization.

Africa is also a rich continent in terms of its flora and fauna. This continent is home to the magnificent lions, the tall giraffes, the grand African elephants, the fast cheetahs, the gorillas, hippos and many more forms of wild life. It is after all here that you can see thousands of flamingos standing together near a lake. Do you know that Africa has more than 3000 protected areas across the continent!

Do you know that Africa falls in all the four hemispheres! The spectacular landscapes of Sahara can leave its visitor spellbound. Mount Kilimanjaro is the highest point in Africa and Lake Victoria is the largest lake in Africa. Interestingly, the equator also crosses the African continent. Despite all that can be written about Africa, words cannot capture the essence of Africa. It is a vast continent, where people following various beliefs live, a continent where the spirit of the people living here will entice and fascinate you. It is a land of contrasts that will make you visit Africa again and again.

Let's remember the story

Answer the following questions.

1. Which oceans and seas surround the African continent?
2. It is said that it was in Africa that the human beings had evolved. Explain.
3. Which ancient civilization had evolved in Africa?
4. Which is the most populous country and city in Africa?
5. Who was 'Lucy'?
6. What do you know about the wildlife in Africa?

Crossword

With the help of given clues, complete the crossword.

Across

1. Remain of animals and man buried in earth
2. An animal with long legs and long neck

Down

3. Longest river
4. Largest desert
5. Land of an old civilization

Match the idioms given in Column A with their meanings in Column B.

Column A	Column B
The lion's share	A rehearsal
Get over it	To make someone laugh
Haste makes wastes	To move beyond something that is troubling you
Dry run	The biggest portion of something
A night owl	Quickly done things lead to poor ending
Crack someone up	Staying up late at night

Monument talk

Find out with the help of your teacher about some of the famous places/monuments in Africa. Write a short paragraph on any two places/monuments.

....

....

....

....

....

....

....

....